WHO IS
ZAYNAB?

WHO IS ZAYNAB?

Hajjah Chahnaz A. Kbaisi-Hazari

I.M.A.M.

IMAM MAHDI ASSOCIATION OF MARJAEYA

Imam Mahdi Association of Marjaeya, Dearborn,
MI 48124, www.imam-us.org
©2021 by Imam Mahdi Association of Marjaeya
All rights reserved. Published 2021.
Printed in the United States of America.

ISBN-13: 978-0-9997877-9-3

Contents

Contents

Foreword

In the Name of God, the Most Beneficent,
the Most Merciful

All praise is to God and may His salutations be upon
Prophet Muhammad and his pure progeny

There is no doubt that women have a unique presence, unparalleled status, and remarkable role in human history, despite often difficult and unfavorable circumstances that left them obscured and exposed to different kinds of trials and difficulties. The Holy Quran has provided us with exquisite and wonderful examples of great women who played pivotal and extraordinary roles in the service of God's religion, His prophets, and His chosen ones. For example, the Quran reminds us of the mother of Musa (p), who God distinguished by speaking to her through a divine revelation saying, "We inspired Musa's mother saying, 'Breast-feed your son. When you become afraid for his life, throw him into the sea. Do not be afraid or grieved for We shall return him to you and make him a messenger'".[1] Moreover, it also reminds us of the role

---

1. The Holy Quran, 28:7

of Musa's sister, who was assigned an important secret mission to follow and keep track of her infant brother, "She told Musa's sister to follow her brother. His sister watched him from one side and the people of the Pharaoh did not notice her presence."[2] This mother and sister [of Musa] are a valuable example of great women who were entrusted with the crucial task of ensuring the success of God's plan.

Similarly, we see the same example in the story of the Virgin Maryam (p) who was chosen to carry the "word of God", which was His miracle and brilliant sign Prophet Isa (p). God says about her, "We made the son of Maryam and his mother a miracle and settled them on a high land, quite secure and watered by a spring."[3] Then, in the time of the Holy Quran's revelation, profound and exceptional personalities emerged who followed in the footsteps of those Godly women in the service of religion and the righteous [servants of God] and performed roles that are the object of admiration and astonishment until now because of the strength of belief and adherence to lofty principles. They are lauded because they represent great ideals and values, exhibit patience and bear trials, and face various circumstances and difficulties. These qualities have made them into role models and a beacon of ideal

---

2. The Holy Quran, 28:11

3. The Holy Quran, 23:50

character in every condition. Zaynab (p) is one of these great ladies!

Al-Hawra Zaynab accepted, carried out, and fulfilled the task entrusted to her with grace and in the best manner. Zaynab (p) shared in the imamate's mission of reform with Imam Hussain (p) to resist corruption, prevent the humiliation of Islam after the death of the Holy Prophet (pbuh&hp), and stop the deviation of Muslims from the way of his holy family. Thus, just as Imam Hussain's role was to sacrifice and give of himself for the pleasure of God, Zaynab's task was to fight tyranny and stand against injustice with her eloquent words, unwavering stand, perseverance, and patience under the severest of circumstances. Had it not been for her eye-opening speeches that fearlessly declared the truth, exposed the reality of what had transpired, and revealed the horrors and scandal of the enemy and their devious plan, Imam Hussain's movement would not be remembered today.

Islam does not differentiate between the role of women and men in the fulfillment of duties to God and humanity. In fact, they are both the same. God says, "The believers, both male and female, are each other's guardians. They try to make others do good, prevent them from committing sins, perform their prayers, pay the religious tax, and obey God and His Messenger. God will have mercy on them; He is Majestic and All-wise."[4] As such, there is no preference for one over the other,

---

4. The Holy Quran, 9:71

male or female, except by one of four things. It is either by faith or knowledge, as God says, "God will raise the position of the believers and of those who have received knowledge"[5], or as God states about piety, "The most honorable among you in the sight of God is the most pious of you"[6], or regarding good deeds, "All righteously believing male or female will be granted a blessed happy life and will receive their due reward and more."[7]

Hence, any discussion about the difference between males and females cannot be founded on anything except understanding their functional roles. God Almighty bestowed on His creation functions for men and functions for women according to a wisdom that He willed, whether we perceive it or not. Just as it is not possible to measure the difference and give preference to the role of the heart over the liver, or the eye over the ear, or the hand over the leg, the same is true for every creation of God because they have a specific function. Similarly, it is not possible to conflate the role and responsibility of a father, daughter, husband, wife, brother, or sister with another. Furthermore, these unique roles and positions result in specific rights when it comes to things like inheritance, blood money (*diya*), and other important matters. Unfortunately, some use this as an opportunity for libel as a result of their ignorance of the wise Islamic system of religion

---

5. The Holy Quran, 58:11

6. The Holy Quran, 49:13

7. The Holy Quran, 16:97

that guarantees the happiness of believers who implement it in this world and reap its benefits in the hereafter. Otherwise, the essence is one, as is the divine mission behind creation. God said, "People, We have created you all male and female and have made you nations and tribes so that you would recognize each other. The most honorable among you in the sight of God is the most pious of you. God is All-knowing and All-aware."[8]

What the contemporary world is witnessing today in terms of the deteriorating condition of women, and what is cited from many sources, is a truth that raises concern and indicates a misunderstanding of the [high] value and important role of women. Women are often not treated as human beings who deserves full rights. Instead, they are oppressed and mistreated worldwide. Women still constitute the majority of farmers in the world while owning a smaller proportion of the land. Women are the leading healthcare providers, yet they are not always a priority for treatment. Women are still the most affected by wars and conflicts, but they are the least included in arbitrations. Indeed, even with the rise of a global culture of accountability, particularly for those who are violent towards women, violence against women is still prevalent in the world. Women are still subjected to assault, rape, and forced into servitude and demeaning roles, and what is worse is that happens in plain sight for everyone to witness.

---

8. The Holy Quran, 49:13

One of the most important things that will help the contemporary woman recover and affirm her identity as someone who can carry the responsibility placed on humankind as inheritors of Islamic legacy and exercise her divinely apportioned role in educating others, nurturing love and tenderness, as well as facing the injustice, oppression, marginalization and persecution humanity is subjected to, is for them to work hard, day and night, to:

1. Shun ignorance and embrace awareness, knowledge, culture, and everything that is a source of success.
2. Prioritize the goals and interests of life to be realistic and truly valuable, not shallow and only based on material gain.
3. Adhere to heavenly values of belief, behavior, action, morals, knowledge, and purification of the soul and mind.
4. Contemplate and reflect on the holy ladies who changed history and accomplished successes that brought humankind from lowliness to the heights of glory and dignity, as we see in the character of Zaynab (p).

During this time, values have deteriorated and immoralities have prevailed, and women are often reduced to humiliation and lowliness, used for despicable and disrespectful goals that are not worthy of them as the inheritors of Islam's hallowed legacy on earth, nor the role that God wanted for them as described in the Quran and exemplified in the era of the Prophet Muhammad (pbuh&hp). Therefore, we hope and wish for all the girls and young women of this time to return to the study of these great women and reflect on their lives and roles so that contemporary women can regain their position and take the appropriate leading role alongside men, either as a mother, sister, daughter, or wife. Indeed, women are equal partners as they are half of society, and there is no life without them. As a result, women will then be an integral part of the promised heavenly plan to spread equity and justice at the end of time when the awaited Mahdi (may God hasten his return) will appear. It has been narrated from Jabir al-Jufi that Imam al-Baqir (p) said that women will have global leading roles in the era of the Mahdi's advent. He said, "Three hundred and a few more than ten people will gather for him in Mecca, just like the number of companions who fought at Badr, and among them will be fifty women".[9]

Hence, the only way to achieve this lofty goal is to seek guidance from those holy ladies whose lives and achievements are described in the sacred books or described by the words of the righteous chosen ones. Among the most prominent is the al-Hawra Lady Zaynab (p), the daughter of Ali bin Abi Talib (p) and Lady Fatima al-Zahra (p), the daughter of Muhammad (pbuh&hp), the Messenger of God. In this concise and condensed booklet, the respected reader will learn about aspects of her life, accomplishments, struggle in the way of God, and sacrifices for His religion. It has been carefully written

---

9. *Tafsir al-Ayashi*, Vol. 1, page 65, hadith 117; al-Ikhtisas, Shaykh al-Tabarsi, page 285

to highlight the most important and prominent details that we need to know about Zaynab (p), which will motivate the reader to dive deeper into learning about her.

On behalf of myself and everyone at I.M.A.M., I extend my heartfelt gratitude to the author, our esteemed sister, Mrs. Chahnaz Kbaisi-Hazari, for coming up with the idea for this booklet and completing this wonderful work, which complements our previous "Who is Hussain?" publication. This booklet was truly needed and now it is in our hands. Moreover, while I congratulate her for this sincere and generous effort, I am not surprised by her accomplishment because she is one of those modern-day women who is really trying to play the role of a contemporary Zaynabi, whether at home as a mother and wife, in society as a teacher and educator, or in her role to spread knowledge and heritage, like writing and publishing, so she can fulfill some of the roles that God has entrusted to her in the best way. I extend my sincere appreciation to her and wish her success and continued opportunities to contribute in God's way, and that she becomes a role model for all her peers, mothers, wives, teachers, educators, and activists who serve religion and humanity. Let this be an open invitation to all believing women who find in themselves the desire and capability of providing a service in the way of God and human advancement, to take the initiative because they will find that I.M.A.M.'s doors are open for collaboration, and to provide assistance, support, and guidance as much as God Almighty wills for it to exercise its leadership and pioneering role in serving the community of believers in the West.

Finally, and certainly not least, I extend my thanks and appreciation to all the individuals who worked on this booklet including the peer reviewers, editors, graphic designers, technical experts, and administrators who exerted their continuous efforts in preparing this booklet and making it available for our valued readers. May the peace, mercy, and blessings of God be upon you.

Sayyid M. B. Kashmiri
Jurist-representative

Chapter 1

············•◆•············

Introduction

God has instilled a boundless potential within each human being to spread goodness and resist evil and corruption, and although every person is born with this basic nature, Islam exhorts Muslims to consciously cultivate and implement these qualities. God says in the Holy Quran, "Let there be a group among you who will invite others to do good deeds, command them to obey the Law, and prohibit them from committing sins."[10] Islam established this code of practice with the message of Prophet Muhammad (pbuh&hp), not only by promulgating a complete set of divine laws and a system of practice, but also by providing a shining example of the highest human morality, ethics, and character in the Prophet.Upholding these lofty ideals, both during the time of the Prophet and after he left this world, fell on the shoulders of faithful, sincere, and righteous men and women. Although it is falsely proposed by some people that only men were, and continue to be, the supporters of this divine cause, it is clear from

---

10. The Holy Quran, 3:104

the Holy Quran and quite honestly, historical evidence, that women played a crucial role in propagating Islam, establishing its equitable social foundation, and resisting corruption and moral decay in society. Prior to the advent of Islam, women had no rights in a society that was predominantly governed by tribal laws. They could not own property or seek positions of social or political leadership. Rather, they were often considered property themselves, sometimes even passed from father to son (i.e., as if by inheritance) upon the former's demise.[11] One of the more heinous crimes against women during this period was the killing of many infant or adolescent girls at the hands of their fathers because of the perceived burden upon the family. About this the Holy Quran asks, "questions are asked about the baby girls buried alive, such as, 'For what crime were they murdered?'"[12]

These disparities were not just restricted to the pre-Islamic Arabian peninsula; the laws of the Roman and Byzantine empires treated women like second-class citizens as they restricted or prohibited them from owning or having disposal over property, and even considered them to be the property of men in some instances.[13] Today, there are some communities and

---

11. Haifaa Jawad, *The Rights of Women in Islam*

12. The Holy Quran, 81:8-9

13. Smith, Bonnie G (2008). *The Oxford Encyclopedia of Women in World History: 4 Volume Set*. London, UK: Oxford University Press, pages 440 – 442

cultural traditions, sadly even among Muslims, that perpetuate these backward ways and continue to stifle the potential of women and relegate them to menial tasks because they are not considered capable of changing society or directly addressing its deficits. The responsibility of building a balanced, just, and compassionate society falls on the shoulders of both men and women even today. Indeed, the Holy Quran points to the fact that people, men and women, are the inheritors of the earth and as such, bear the obligation of stewardship: "On earth, We have made each of your generations the successors of their predecessors; We have made some of you do good deeds of a higher degree than others. He will test you in this way through what He has revealed to you."[14] Hence, in general, Islam calls upon both men and women to lead the way in doing good and resisting evil, act as role models, and maintain higher standards. Men and women are considered equally capable in the execution of this divine directive, and together represent an unwavering instrument of change. The Holy Quran describes these believers "...who left their homes and strove for the cause of God, through their property and in person and those who gave refuge to them and helped them will be each other's guardians"[15] and "...both male and female, are each other's guardians. They try to make others do good, prevent them from committing sins, perform

---

14. The Holy Quran, 6:165

15. The Holy Quran, 8:72

their prayers, pay the religious tax, and obey God and His Messenger. God will have mercy on them; He is Majestic and All-wise."[16]

---

16. The Holy Quran, 9:71

Chapter 2

················◆·◆················

The Women who Supported Islam in the Early Days of the Prophetic Mission

There were many honorable women who openly accepted the word of God and became Muslims, and as a result, faced many difficulties while supporting Prophet Muhammad (pbuh&hp). These devoted women struggled for God's religion and sacrificed what was dearest to them to defend Islam. This included women like Sumayyah, the mother of Ammar bin Yaser, Fatima bint Asad, the mother of Imam Ali (p), Safiyyah bint Abd al-Muttalib, and many others. Women have sacrificed for God and His religion throughout the ages and in various ways. The most distinguished of the women who gave in the cause of Islam, defended its foundation and sacred tenets, and served as unmatched role models were Lady Khadija (p), Lady Fatima (p), and Lady Zaynab (p). They represented the best of Islam and continue to be its best examples, even today.

Khadija bint Khuwaylid (p)

Prophet Muhammad's entire mission was fraught with trials and difficulties. Yet, the early days posed a particular challenge. Preaching to the pagans of Quraysh was an immense task by itself, but to do so with only a handful of supporters, especially given the continuous scheming and machinations against him, made it that much harder. Despite belonging to the prominent tribe of Banu Hashim, who were Quraysh's chiefs, and having an uncle whose position among the Arabs was unparalleled in terms of influence, Prophet Muhammad (pbuh&hp) was still subjected to abuse and torture on a daily basis. Even his marriage to the "Princess of Arabia" and his affiliation with her did not shield him from the constant assault at the hands of the Qurayshi pagans. There is no question that Lady Khadija (p) was a believer in the oneness of God or *muwahhid* (i.e., she was not an idol-worshipper) and that she had significant wealth and social standing. Yet the events of the first night of revelation and the succeeding years revealed the extent of that belief and her lofty status and demonstrated her unwavering and complete support for her husband, and as such, the message of God. It is reported that she once said to the ladies of Mecca before her marriage to Prophet Muhammad (pbuh&hp), "Do you not see that this man has a great status? Do you not see him standing alone with a shade [constantly] over his head, it moves where he moves and stops when he stops, and covers him from the heat and cold [wherever he is]?"[17] As Imam Hussain (p) is reported to have said to the enemy soldiers in Karbala, "Don't you know that my grandmother Khadija daughter of Khuwaylid was the first lady of this ummah to become a Muslim?"[18] Thus, she supported the Prophet when there was no one else by his side except Ali. She not only cared for him personally, but gave all of her extensive possessions to him and the cause of Islam.

Many years later, the Prophet is quoted to have said to one of his other wives, "she believed in me when everyone considered me a liar, she supported me with [her] wealth when everyone deprived me."[19] This was particularly apparent during the three years when Quraysh boycotted the Prophet's tribe in a desolate ravine. Lady Khadija (p) gave every last bit of what she owned and possessed to sustain the people who were under siege, especially the children, so much so that when she died the Prophet did not have enough money for a proper shroud to wrap and bury her in. The year of her death, which was the same year in which his uncle Abu Talib passed away, was a period of such loss for the Prophet that it became known as the year of sorrow.

---

17. al-Hidaya al-Kubra, Hussain ibn Hamdan, pages 51-54

18. al-Amali, Shaykh al-Saduq, page 222

19. Rawdat al-Waidheen, al-Nishapuri, page 269

Fatima al-Zahra bint Muhammad (p)

The Holy Quran states, "Among the believers, those who stay at home without a good reason are not equal to those who strive for the cause of God in person or with their property. To those who strive for His cause in person or with their property, God has granted a higher rank than to those who stay at home. God has promised that everyone will receive his proper share of the reward but He will grant a much greater reward to those striving for His cause than to those who stay home (for no reason)"[20], and thus, "all righteously believing male or female will be granted a blessed happy life and will receive their due reward and more."[21] Thus, can any person question the importance of those people who supported the Prophet from the very start of his mission, including pious and valiant ladies like Sumayyah, the mother of Ammar son of Yasir, who was one of the first martyrs of Islam with her husband?

Similarly, there was one young girl who supported the message of God in those early days by caring for her father and tending to his needs as a mother would to her children. For this reason, she was known as *Umm abeeha*[22] or the "mother of her father". Just like her mother, Lady Fatima's care for her father was not just

---

20. The Holy Quran, 4:95

21. The Holy Quran, 16:97

22. Bihar al-Anwar, Vol. 43, page 19

an affection due to kinship, rather it was attentiveness towards God's Prophet and the safeguarding of His message because the Holy Quran testifies, "Muhammad is not the father of any of your males. He is the Messenger of God and the last Prophet".[23] When pagans like Abu Jahl threw rubbish on the Prophet, Fatima always hurried to wipe it away. In Mecca, she shielded his body from the stones and consoled him during the unrelenting verbal abuse. Thus, her support for the Messenger and the spread of Islam were unparalleled, and it did not fade as the years progressed and the Muslims gained greater security in Madina. In the battle of Uhud, when news of the Prophet's injury reached Madina, Fatima came out to the battlefield and tended to her father's wounds.[24]

The love of the Prophet for his daughter was expressed not only by his words but by his gestures and customary practices. His statement, "Fatima is a piece of me, whoever angers her has angered me"[25] is unanimously accepted among Muslims and there is no objection to the fact that she was the most beloved to him. Fatima was the last person he would visit before departing for an expedition or travel and she was the first person he would go to upon his return.[26] This love extended to her children, Hasan, Hussain, Zaynab, and Umm

---

23. The Holy Quran, 33:40

24. *Safinatul Bihar*, Abbas Qummi, Vol. 1, page 140

25. *Sahih Bukhari*, Vol. 3, page 1144

26. Bihar al-Anwar, Vol. 43, page 83

Kulthum, who were his only grandchildren and who grew up in his house and surrounded by his holy character and love.

Lineage of Zaynab bint Ali (p)

Zaynab (p) was the daughter of Imam Ali ibn Abi Talib (p), who was the son of Abu Talib and Fatima, daughter of Asad, and Lady Fatima al-Zahra (p) who was the daughter of Prophet Muhammad (pbuh&hp) and Lady Khadija, daughter of Khuwaylid (p). Her lineage dates back directly to Prophet Ibrahim (p) and his son Ismail (p). It is accepted by the majority of Muslims that Zaynab's forefathers from the side of Prophet Muhammad were all believers in the oneness of God and adhered to the *sharia* of Prophet Ibrahim (p). In addition, history documents that they were the trusted leaders of Quraysh and the custodians of the Ka'aba dating back to Qusay, the fourth ancestor of the Prophet. They were known to serve the people and had a reputation of generosity, kindness and benevolence. Abdul Muttalib, the Prophet's grandfather, was especially recognized for his justice and equity and fidelity to God. When Abraha Ashram, the Ethiopian general, threatened Mecca and the Ka'aba, Abdul Muttalib descended towards the door of the Ka'aba, held onto its ropes and proclaimed, "O Allah! We do not depend on anyone except You in our faith, [and] in remaining safe from their mischief and harm. O Lord! Prevent them from reaching your Sanctuary. This enemy of the Ka'aba is hostile to You. O Nourisher! Cut off their hands so that they may not violate Your house. My own property is my right, so I am endeavoring for its safety. However, the safety of Your house is Your responsibility. Do not let that day come when their creed becomes victorious over it, and the people of their lands encroach [with their ways] upon Your land and conquer it".[27] Thus, the deep sincerity to God, service in His way and dependence on Him was a cardinal characteristic of the Prophet's family, ancestors and descendants. These values were carried forward from Mecca to Madina when the Prophet sought to establish the Islamic nation.

Birth, Childhood, And Upbringing in the House of Infallibility

In Madina, the Prophet of Islam founded a society based on brother- and sisterhood, and fostered the bond of faith by building the mosque that would bear his name and serve as the place where all Muslims would gather for congregational prayer. It also became a central location such that the houses of the believers had easy access to it. Although it held the significance of a spiritual palace among the people, the childhood home of Zaynab (p), which was known as *Bayt al-isma*, was in actuality just a simple residence adjoining the Mosque of the Prophet with its south wall measuring approximately 14.5 m in length, its north wall 14 m, and its width on the east and west sides at about

---

27. Shaykh Jafar Subhani, The Message,

5.7 m.[28] Moreover, historians recount that Prophet Muhammad (pbuh&hp) used to perform night prayers (*tahajjud*) in a prayer niche right beside the door of Fatima al-Zahra (p),[29] which was directly connected to the mosque. Similarly, Fatima's prayer niche was located not far from her father's. Thus, the people of this house embodied the loftiest and most complete form of worship to God and devotion to His religion.

This was the house that God chose for Zaynab (p), where she grew up immersed in the prophetic mission of her grandfather and the light of his message. She was born on the 5th of Jamadi al-Awal five years after the prophet's migration, or *hijrah,* from Mecca to Madina (October 2, 626 C.E.) in a house where "...God has declared to be highly respected and His Name be mentioned therein in glory in the morning and evening".[30] It is reported that when asked about the houses mentioned in this verse, the Holy Prophet said, "[They are] the houses of the prophets (pbut), and he extended his hand [to point] towards the house of Fatima (p)".[31] As such, she flourished in the lap of

---

28. Muhammad Labib al-Batnuni, Journey to Hijaz, page 250-251 (1938)

29. Ali ibn Ahmad al-Samhudi, Wafa al-Wafa bi Akhbar Dar al-Mustafa, 2:467

30. The Holy Quran, 24:36 (فِي بُيُوتٍ أَذِنَ اللَّهُ أَن تُرْفَعَ وَيُذْكَرَ فِيهَا اسْمُهُ) (يُسَبِّحُ لَهُ فِيهَا بِالْغُدُوِّ وَالْآصَالِ)

31. Bihar al-Anwar, Majlisi Vol. 23, page 326 (بيوت الأنبياء، وأومأ) (بيده إلى منزل فاطمة عليها السلام)

prophethood and infallibility, surrounded by the divine inspiration of her grandfather, which was the source of all goodness for this household, the nurturing of her father and mother, and the tenderness of her brothers. The members of this house were known for their complete knowledge, mercy, compassion, and devotion to God, and most importantly, the role model status that they fulfilled with full fidelity. Thus, it is no surprise that when one learns about her, they witness her greatness, the impactful role she played, and her legacy to preserve the foundations of belief and the values of human civilization.

Zaynab (p) in the Society of Madina

There is no doubt that society plays a role in the upbringing of every individual such that they develop characteristics not inherited or learned from the parents. This is particularly important in the early years of a person's life when their heart is, as Imam Ali (p) describes, "a fertile land that will grow anything that is planted".[32] These moments shape not only their physical and emotional development, but also determine the resilience with which they face the rigors of life. Zaynab (p) grew up in the society of Madina under the leadership of Prophet Muhammad (pbuh&hp), who transformed it from a collection of independent tribes bound together by decades-old allegiances and ignorant practices into a torch of civilization for all nations

---

32. The will of Imam Ali (p)

of the world. From this society, in which Prophet Muhammad (pbuh&hp) sowed the roots of brotherhood, cooperation, and equality, arose great heroes like Salman, Abu Dharr and Ammar. Although this first Islamic society was built on all these great qualities, it must be acknowledged that there remained a pull of the old tribal ways of social and racial hierarchy, hegemony, and blood restitution that would carry on after the demise of the Prophet and would challenge the egalitarian philosophy of Islam, and as a result, create friction, misappropriation of resources, and bloodshed. This was undoubtedly rooted in the greed for power and influence over a growing and ever-expanding nation that was quickly incorporating new lands and acquiring wealth.

In Madina, Zaynab (p) witnessed the early years of the Islamic nation and she surely understood the dynamics of the world she found herself in because of her grandfather and father's prominent roles. Moreover, despite the fact that many past enemies like Abu Sufyan and his son Muawiya were declaring themselves to be Muslim, at least on the surface, enmity against the Prophet and his family remained deeply entrenched in the hearts of many. Yet, political expediency demanded that these enemies feign being Muslim to position themselves for an eventual takeover. Therefore, Zaynab (p) was not like any other child her age, she was not occupied by the childish and worldly things and showed great maturity from a young age. It is narrated that one day her father sat her down in his lap and asked her to say 'one', and she did. Then, he asked her to say 'two', but she did not respond. So, Imam Ali (p) coaxed her, "speak my beloved child". She then said, "O' my father, I cannot say 'two' with the same tongue I said 'one'". He hugged her tight and kissed her.[33] This was proof of her extraordinary intelligence and deep understanding of faith, despite her young age; she observed and grasped what was happening around her.

Trials from a Young Age

The trials and tribulations that a person faces in life make them who they are and their lesson remains imprinted on them through the years. It is reported that when Zaynab (p)was born, her grandfather came to see her. He took her in his arms and held her close to his cheek and then began to weep. Lady Fatima (p) asked, "what has made you cry my father, may God never allow your eyes to weep?" He replied, "My daughter, O' Fatima, know that this girl will be tested with severe misfortunes and heartbreaking catastrophe after you and I have left this world". Hearing this, Fatima (p) also wept and she asked, "what is the reward for those who weep for her and the difficulties she experiences?". The Prophet replied, "O' Fatima, my dear, the reward for those who weep for her and the

---

33. Shajarat Toobah, Muhammad Mahdi al-Hairi, vol. 2, page 392

difficulties she faces is the [same] reward for weeping for her brother [Hussain]".[34]

Thus, as Imam Ali (p) is reported to have said, "In the life experiences we face is a knowledge that is continuous [through life]."[35] Zaynab (p) was only five years old when she faced her first trial, the loss of her beloved grandfather, the Holy Prophet of Islam. It was his holy presence that had been sheltering the family, because they were honored and revered while he was alive, and the hypocrites dared not make any advances against them. The city of Madina was shaken by his demise and there was uncertainty in the Muslim nation. Yet, the most profound sense of loss was experienced in the house of Fatima (p). One wonders what Zaynab (p) must have felt as her mother, father and brothers hung onto the Prophet as his blessed life faded. How must she have felt watching her mother mourn the immense loss? As if to foreshadow her actions decades later, Fatima (p) took a handful of earth from the grave of her father, placed it on her eyes and said, "Anyone who smells the fragrance of the earth of Ahmad has lost nothing if they never smell any other [pleasing] fragrance. What misfortunes have fallen

---

34. Al-Khassais al-Zaynabia, Sayyid Nuradeen al-Jazairi, page 33

35. Bihar al-Anwar, Majlisi Majlisi Vol. 71, page 342 (في التجارب علم مستأنف)

upon me [after you], if they had fallen upon the daytime, they would turn it into night."[36]

In the midst of this pain, the society of Madina was in further disharmony because of the looming political conflict between the *Muhajireen* or the immigrants who fled Mecca and adopted Madina as their home, and the *Ansar* or the native residents of Madina who invited the Prophet. The efforts of the Prophet to build brotherhood in the fledgling Islamic nation were being tested as those with ulterior motives saw their opportunity to subvert the divine mandate and seize power. As Zaynab's family was busy preparing for the Prophet's burial, a small number of prominent members of society hastily met at a shed or *saqifah* used by the Saidah tribe to decide who would succeed him as the leader of the nation. Although most who were gathered there eventually agreed to the final choice, there were strong disagreements, even to the point of violence, between certain Muhajireen and Ansar. More importantly, Zaynab's father Ali, who was raised by the Prophet and was the first person to stand with him and who had defended Islam from the very first day, was not present. Confirmation, and to some degree legitimization, of the final choice needed his approval, or at least his acquiescence by way of a pledge of allegiance.[37]

---

36. Masnad Ahmad, vol. 2, page 489

37. The Succession of Muhammad, Wilfred Madelung, page 32

Therefore, shortly after the Prophet's funeral, the new administration sought Ali's allegiance, which represented the tacit approval of the Bani Hashim, the tribe of the Holy Prophet and Imam Ali (p).[38] When the allegiance was not given, the narrations and reports state that the administration's agents rushed to the "door of Fatima" to force Imam Ali (p) to pledge allegiance and unequivocally accept the leadership that was decided upon at saqifah.[39,40] Despite the aggressive demands, the door of Fatima (p) remained closed, when finally the threat of burning the house was announced to the household of the Prophet. When Fatima (p) asked, "will you burn the door [of my home] upon me?", the agent replied, "yes, this will strengthen the faith brought to us by your father".[41,42] The notorious actions were carried out to the extent that Fatima (p) was crushed behind the door causing her to miscarry her unborn child Muhsin.[43] This is the same Fatima about who the Prophet said, "Fatima is a part of me. Whoever makes her angry, makes me

---

38. Muhammad in History, Thought, and Culture: An Encyclopedia of the Prophet of God, Coeli Fitzpatrick and Adam Hani Walker, page 3

39. History of al-Tabari, vol. 1, pages 1118-1120

40. History of ibn al-Athir, vol. 2, page 325

41. Ansab al-Ashraf, al-Baladhuri, vol. 1, pages 582-586. (أتراك
((محرقاً عليّ بابي)؟ قال : نعم ، وذلك أقوى ممّا جاء به أبوك

42. Kanz al-Ummal, vol. 3, page 140

43. Wafi al-Wafiyat, Salahudin Khalil al-Safadi, vol. 6, page 76 ()

angry".[44] It is unknown whether Zaynab (p) was in the house at the time of the assault or whether she witnessed the brutal attack on her mother. However, it is incontrovertible that Fatima (p) was severely injured, became sick and died soon thereafter, refusing to speak to the khalifah or the agents who perpetrated the assault.[45] How does a girl of five years cope with such a calamity and deal with the loss of her mother so soon after losing her beloved grandfather? Her future actions show that she learned from her mother's immovable resolve and unrelenting opposition to injustice.

Despite the trials, the family of the Prophet continued to advocate for truth and justice and the preservation of religion after his demise. Zaynab (p) witnessed her mother step out of her home and enter the Mosque of the Prophet to affirm the proof set forth by her father and shed light on the tenets of faith and the proper ways of practice when the directives of Islam were being confounded. She said, "Faith has been ordained to cleanse you of polytheism, prayers are prescribed to keep you away from pride, *zakat* (charity) has been prescribed to purify you and results in the increase of sustenance; fasting has been prescribed so that sincerity may be reinforced, *hajj* (pilgrimage) has been prescribed to establish the religion, and justice is

---

44. Sahih Bukhari, vol. 3, hadith 1144 (فاطمة بضعة مني، فمن أغضبها فمن أغضبني)

45. Al-Imamah wa al-Siyasah, ibn Qutaybah, vol. 1, page 14

prescribed to establish proper harmony in the hearts."
Moreover, she reminded all who were gathered and
everyone in history who she was, and as a result, the
significance of her (i.e., the Prophet's) progeny,
declaring, "the obligation to obey us (the *Ahlul Bayt*)
has been prescribed to set up order in the community,
and our authority (*imamate*) has been prescribed to
save the people from differences. O' people! Know that
I am Fatima and my father was Muhammad. I say and I
will repeat this again and again and I do not utter any
falsehood, and whatever I do shall not be wrong.
'Indeed an Apostle from among yourselves has come to
you, grievous to him is your falling into distress, (he is)
solicitous regarding your welfare, towards the faithful
(he is) compassionate, (and) merciful'.[46] If you observe
and understand, you will find that this prophet is my
father and not the father of any one of your women; he
is the brother of my cousin [Ali] and not the brother of
any one of your men and how fortunate is the one
related to him (the Prophet)."

The seriousness of this action is underscored by the
fact that Lady Fatima (p) would seldom, if ever, venture
into public, ensuring that she was hidden from the eyes
of strangers. Thus, Muslims acknowledge the weight of
her speech because it represents one of the most
valuable lessons in history, from a man or a woman.
This was an indelible mark on the young Zaynab (p)
who adopted the chastity of her mother and wielded

---

46. The Holy Quran, 9:128

the power of truth and eloquence. As such, the stand of Fatima (p) and Zaynab (p) decades later, was a bold rebuke against those who saw women as weak and lacking in any sort of will to create change in society. Furthermore, it was a courageous refusal to be silenced and submit to the standards of ignorance which actively sought to marginalize anyone who did not fit the hierarchy.

Approximately six months after the demise of the Holy Prophet, Zaynab (p) witnessed the death of her mother who was only 18 years of age. The passing of Fatima continued the sorrows in the household of the Prophet and it must have forced Zaynab (p) to take on responsibilities that were bigger than her five years of age. Once again, this followed in the legacy of her mother who was known as *Umm abeeha* or the "mother of her father" because of the way she cared for her father after the death of Fatima (p) while still a young girl. Zaynab (p) must have assumed such a role to care for her father, brothers and sister, especially her brother Hussain, from whom she became inseparable. As if all of these trials were a preparation for what she would face in the future, which would be a summation of the duty of her life.

Zaynab the Educator

As the religion of Islam spread in the Arabian peninsula, there was an increasing need for people to know and understand true Islamic values and rules, especially as the religion began to reach more distant places (i.e., away from Mecca and Madina) where the cultures and traditions started to blend in with religious traditions and practices. In those days, women did not normally hold prominent social roles, particularly when it came to administration, leadership, or even education. Yet, Islam emphasized the mutual duty of both men and women in upholding the tenets and teachings of Islam. From the early days, beginning with the migration from Mecca to Madina, it was a role that both women and men took part in as they supported the cause of the Prophet of Islam.

Islam has obligated every Muslim to seek education, and as such, men and women should strive to learn. The Holy Prophet is reported to have said, "seeking knowledge is an obligation upon every Muslim".[47] By virtue of this directive, Islam opened the door for women to learn and become educators. The worth of this action is equally weighed and rewarded for both sexes: Allah states, "Their Lord answered their prayers saying, "I do not neglect anyone's labor whether the laborer be male or female. You are all related to one another".[48] It is by virtue of knowledge and reasoning that the prophets (pbut) guided their communities, and in this regard Prophet Muhammad (pbuh&hp) said, "God would not send any prophet or messenger until their minds were complete, and their minds were

---

47. Bihar al-Anwar, vol. 2. Page 32

48. The Holy Quran, 3:195

superior to the minds of their community members".[49] So how must it have been the mind [and knowledge] of the greatest of all prophets (pbut) and messengers, and accordingly, the minds of the people who were raised in his home and directly under his tutelage? Thus, knowledge was the beacon that pointed to the legitimate leadership and position of Lady Fatima (p) and Zaynab (p) and their role as a source of education to help anchor Islam in the hearts of the believers and spread its teachings to those who still did not know. It is reported that Zaynab (p) would teach the women of Kufah the Holy Quran, the sciences of hadith, theology and ethics after her father moved his administration there from Madina.[50] It is also noted that at times the narrators would turn to her for clarification on certain matters that were unclear. Zaynab (p) was also described by her nephew Imam Ali ibn Hussain (p) who said, "my aunt, you are, by the grace of God, a scholar who has not been taught [by anyone else] and one who understands without having to be explained".[51] Moreover, Egyptian historian Hasan Ibrahim Hasan, who specialized in Islamic history, especially the Fatimid period, states, "She [Zaynab] was known to be the most eloquent Arab woman of her time and the most devoted in worship"[52] indicating that her

---

49. Usul al-Kafi, vol. 1, page 12, hadith 11

50. Safeenatul Bihar, Abbas al-Qummi, vol. 1, page 558

51. Al-Ihtijaj, al-Tabarsi, vol. 2, page 31

52. The Role of Women in Islamic History, Hasan Ibrahim Hasan, page 48

knowledge of God and adherence to the truth, as inculcated in her from her family, were beyond what an ordinary person possessed. Hence, she was referred to as *fasihah,* or immaculately fluent, and *baleeghah,* highly eloquent. These very important and essential qualities became the impetus for spreading the divine message and defending the oppressed, because despite all the adversities that she faced, she never abandoned the obligation that was upon the Prophet's family to guide and champion the rights of people.

Marriage and Family Life

Zaynab (p) became known among the people of Madina for her great knowledge, intelligence, and high character; she was, after all, the inheritor of the Prophet, Imam Ali (p) and Lady Fatima (p). Several respected men sought her hand in marriage, but eventually her union was arranged with Abdullah son of Jaffer, who was not only known to be honorable, virtuous and generous, but also came from a family that had sacrificed for the cause of Islam. His father, Jaffer son of Abu Talib, was known as *al-tayyar* or the one who is bestowed wings in heaven because his arms were severed before he was martyred in the battle of Mu'tah. His mother was Asma daughter of Umays who was a close companion of Lady Fatima (p), she was by her side during the birth of Hasan and Hussain and when she departed from this world. Abdullah was the first Muslim born in Ethiopia (*Habasha*) during their asylum there and he fought alongside Imam Ali (p) in the battles of Jamal and Siffeen. Zaynab (p) and Abdullah had four sons: Ali, Abbas, Aun, and Muhammad, and a daughter Umm Kulthum.[53] Zaynab's marriage to Abdullah did not separate her from her father and brothers; she remained very close to them, especially Hussain. Imam Ali (p) was very attached to his beloved daughter who was a living piece of the Prophet and Lady Fatima (p). Zaynab (p) continued to live with her father and she and her husband moved to Kufah with him in 37 A.H. This move was not only due to her love and attachment to her father and brothers. Zaynab (p) was aware of the political changes around her and she wanted to be close to the Imam of the time during his administration of the Muslim ummah.

---

53. Ibn Asakir, *ilam al-nisa*, page 190

Chapter 3

Upholding the Truth and
Safeguarding the Legacy of
the Ahl al-Bayt (p)

When Imam Hussain (p) saw that the enemy
would not desist from their aggression and
assault until he was martyred in Karbala, it
is reported that he gave a number of directives to his
sister Zaynab (p). More importantly, he pointed to her
as the person the family should turn to in that moment
of difficulty. So profound was this position of Zaynab (p)
among the Ahl al-Bayt (p) that it was continuously
mentioned and emulated throughout the years of
persecution under the Umayyads and the Abbasids. In
fact, it is reported that a man once approached Lady
Hakima, the daughter of Imam Jawad (p) and sister of
Imam Hadi (p), who lived during the time of the 9th,
10th, 11th and 12th Imams, to inquire about the final
Imam. After she described his succession and mentioned
his name, the man asked, "Were you a witness to this
matter (i.e., his birth and appointment) or is this
something you have [only] heard?" She answered,
"This is what Abu Muhammad (Imam Askari) has

written to his mother." He asked, "Where is the newborn?", to which she replied, "He is hidden!" So he said, "Who should the Shia turn to [in this matter]?", to which she responded, "They should follow Abu Muhammad's mother." The man then inquired, "Should we follow one who is directed to (i.e., appointed in a will) through a woman?" Lady Hakima answered, "You should follow Hussain son of Ali ibn Abi Talib (p), who gave his testament openly to his sister Zaynab daughter of Ali (p), who was his legatee, and as such, the knowledge that was possessed by Ali son of Hussain (the surviving Imam) (p) was ascribed through Zaynab (p) so that the matter of the Imamate of Ali son of Hussain would remain secret."[54] This points to the critical role played by the ladies of Ahl al-Bayt (p) in preserving the living Imam, and in doing so, safeguarding the message of God. Furthermore, it is reasonable to conclude that had Zaynab (p) not been capable or worthy of such an appointment, Imam Hussain (p) would not have placed such an important task in her hand.

The Plotting of the Umayyads

The Holy Quran states, "When We said to you, 'Indeed your Lord encircles those people,' We did not appoint the vision that We showed you except as a tribulation for the people and the tree cursed in the Quran. We warn them, but it only increases them in their

---

54. *Kamal al-din wa itmam al-nima*, Shaykh al-Saduq, page 501

outrageous rebellion."[55] It is reported that the cursed tree mentioned in this verse refers to the Umayyad family, who sought to sully the Prophet's message and spread corruption.[56] Imam Hussain (p) himself remarked when leaving Madina in Rajab of 60 AH, "Truly we are from God, and to Him will we return, may God save Islam if it is ever led by a [corrupt] shepherd like Yazid. I heard my grandfather say, 'caliphate is prohibited for the family of Abi Sufyan (i.e., the Umayyads)."[57] Indeed, the Umayyad machinations originated before the time of Prophet Muhammad (p); they were unabashedly declared during the early battles, and then came to fruition in the years after his demise, especially after the reign of the third caliph. Thus, it is no surprise that the Ahl al-Bayt (p) were aware of the Umayyad plots and their ulterior motives at every critical moment in those first decades of the Islamic nation. Lady Fatima (p) witnessed this first-hand in the aftermath of the Battle of Uhud when she received news of the inhumane desecration of her uncle Hamza's body by Hind, the wife of Abu Sufyan. In a testament to his bravery and preserving the valor he demonstrated, she made a rosary out of the sand of his grave, as if to foreshadow what would transpire for Zaynab (p) years later.

---

55. The Holy Quran, 17:60

56. al-Durr al-Manthur, al-Suyuti, Vol. 4, page 191; Tarikh al-Tabari, al-Tabari, Vol. 8, page 185.

57. Bihar al-Anwar, al-Majlisi, Vol. 44, page 326

Lady Zaynab (p) was not ignorant of the prevailing currents and the factors that caused unrest among Muslims, especially in the time of her father's caliphate. Muslims turned to him and pledged their allegiance when the third caliph was killed. Although he initially refused to take the office, their persistence and his unceasing desire to preserve Islam eventually caused him to accept. Imam Ali (p) relates, "At that moment (i.e., when the people came to pledge allegiance to him), nothing surprised me with the crowd of people rushing to me. They advanced towards me from every side like the hyenas approach, so much so that Hasan and Hussein were getting crushed and the garment was torn on both ends of my shoulder. They collected around me like a herd of sheep and goats. Thus, when I assumed the responsibility [of the caliphate], one party broke away and another turned disobedient while the rest began acting wrongfully as if they had not heard the word of God, 'There is the life hereafter which We have prepared for those who do not want to impose their superiority over the others in the land nor commit evil therein. The happy end certainly belongs to the pious ones.'"[58]

In all of those moments, Zaynab (p) saw in her father the Prophet's champion who sought to restore justice and equity, and push back against Umayyad nepotism and usurpation of people's rights. In doing so, he inevitably stirred the hatred of those corrupt

---

58. The Holy Quran, 28:83; Nahjul Balagha, Sermon 3

individuals, who stopped at nothing to derail his lofty quest and cause him harm. Indeed, it was the pretense of avenging the third caliph's death that openly revealed the animosity of Muawiyah ibn Abi Sufyan and the Umayyads against the family of the Prophet. Muawiyah had only begrudgingly accepted Islam when the Muslims liberated Mecca and now used the killing of the third caliph as his excuse to attack Imam Ali (p). The chain of events that followed, namely the Battle of Jamal, the Battle of Siffeen and the subsequent schemes during its eventual arbitration, and the Battle of Nahrawan, led to a splintering of the Islamic nation. Zaynab (p) was in her thirties during that period of time and likely realized that those who were sincere, steadfast, and active in the stand for God's true religion and against injustice were very few.

There was also a widespread campaign of disinformation and propaganda against Imam Ali (p) by the Umayyads, who openly cursed him from the pulpits of Damascus. These political moves were very costly to Muslims, and decades of misappropriation had worn away the trust in leadership, both centrally and locally. Zaynab (p) witnessed many of the Prophet's loyal companions speak up against the unjust practices and the abandonment of the prophetic sunnah through the years. Yet, she also saw how those who were bold enough to speak out were dealt with aggression and severity. This included Abu Dharr al-Ghifari who was first banished from Madina to Damascus and then exiled to *Jabal Amil* (present-day south Lebanon).[59] This great companion eventually died alone in Rabadha. Others openly challenged Imam Ali's position as *Amir al-Mumineen,* or leader of the believers, sometimes while lining up behind him in congregational prayers. This group of Muslims, who became known as the Kharijites, accused him of apostasy and engaged in terrorism and extreme violence,[60] all while feigning piety, asceticism, and devotion to the Holy Quran. This group was particularly insidious because of their false puritanical approach to Islam and intolerance.

It was exactly as Imam Ali (p) had predicted when he took the reins of the ummah, one party had broken away [and violated their allegiance], another was disobedient to God's law, and yet another was seditious and corrupt. The kharijites eventually put into motion a plot to assassinate Imam Ali (p), which was carried out by Abdul Rahman ibn Muljam on the 19th of the month of Ramadan in 40 AH. The death of Imam Ali (p) on the 21st of that month was a massive loss to not only the Prophet's family but the whole Islamic nation. Zaynab (p) must have faced that moment with patience and resilience despite the devastating tragedy. Moreover, by then, she must have fully understood the evil intentions that drove people to undermine the lofty

59. Tarikh Yaqubi, Vol. 2, page 148

60. Muslim Rebels: Kharijites and the Politics of Extremism in Egypt. Jeffrey Thomas Kenney, Jeffrey T. Kenney. Oxford University Press, 2006.

goals of Islam and take them to such extremes that it justified the violent killing of her father.

Although Zaynab's brother Hasan (p) was chosen to succeed their father as caliph, he was immediately met with the continued aggression of Muawiyah, who marched against him in the first few months of his caliphate.[61] Like his father, Imam Hasan (p) did not want to engage in a battle or do anything that would lead to the loss of lives, but he could not stand by while a despot like Muawiyah continued to destroy the fabric of Islamic society and the foundations laid down by his grandfather [on which it stood]. Thus, it is related that when he was finally forced to sign a treaty with Muawiyah, Imam Hasan (p) said, "I am not someone who would [ever] dishonor the Muslims, but I was unwilling to have you slaughtered for a kingdom."[62] Zaynab's brother had been abandoned by the vast majority of the soldiers who had pledged to fight by his side, despite the fact that they had pledged their allegiance to him as the caliph. Even his cousin Ubaydallah ibn Abbas, who was the commander of his forces advancing on Muawiyah's army, succumbed to greed and deserted him.[63] Understanding Muawiyah's devious nature and lack of fidelity to the treaty, the family of the Prophet continued to protect and guide Muslims and resist the injustices that had taken root in

---

61. History of the Caliphs, al-Suyuti, page 194.

62. History of the Caliphs, al-Suyuti, page 195.

63. Tarikh al-Yaqubi, Vol. 2, page 191.

much of the Islamic nation at the hands of the Umayyads. In 50 AH, Imam Hasan (p) was poisoned by his wife Jaadah bint al-Ashath who was bribed and eventually betrayed by the Umayyads. This was yet another profound loss for *umm al-masaib* or "the bearer of all misfortunes". Imam Hasan (p) was not only her older brother but also took the place of their beloved father and was certainly the imam of the time. It is reported that Imam Ridha (p) has said, "the older brother is like the father [in his position to the younger siblings]."[64] It seems as if Zaynab (p) was watching and experiencing these events unfold in preparation for the battle and stand of her life. In the treaty, Muawiyah had agreed to abide by the Holy Quran and the true sunnah of the Prophet. He would cease persecution of the Shia, ensure security for all people, especially the companions of the Commander of the Faithful Ali ibn Abi Talib (p), and immediately desist from defaming or praying against him. Moreover, after his demise the authority would automatically go to Imam Hasan (p), and to Hussain ibn Ali (p), Hasan's younger brother, in the event that he had already passed away. The signed treaty also stipulated that Muawiyah would not plot any harm upon Hasan (p) or Hussain (p), nor would he appoint a successor when he neared death.[65] History witnesses that these terms had no significance to Muawiyah, who was morally corrupt and unfaithful to his word, and as such, he proceeded to violate them

64. Bihar al-Anwar, al-Majlisi, Vol. 75, page 335

65. Tarikh al-Tabari, Vol. 6, page 97

with impunity. In fact, it is reported from Said ibn Suwayd that he said, "we were in congregation with Muawiyah for Friday prayers at Nukhayla (i.e., where the treaty with Imam Hasan took place), in his speech he said: 'By God, I did not fight (war) against you so that you uphold your prayers or keep your fasts, or perform pilgrimage or give alms tax (i.e., to preserve its hallowed status among you), you are already doing this! Rather, I fought against you so that I may dominate you [and assume control], and God has given me that while you are loath to accept it."[66]

With Imam Hasan (p) gone, Muawiyah continued his campaign of tyranny and corruption and the Umayyads solidified their hold on the worldly caliphate, which in actuality was more like a monarchy or dictatorship. In the years that followed, many Muslims found themselves in a haze of disillusionment, confusion and an ever-growing distance from the true ethos of Islam. Pursuit of personal gain, worldly accumulation at any cost, and political corruption were rampant. However, the beacon of guidance remained unextinguished because the family of the Prophet continued to illuminate the consciences of their followers and anyone who was seeking the truth. Yet, it seemed inevitable that a major movement was needed to awaken the hearts and minds of all people.

Although viewed as a defeat, or at least a capitulation by many people, the treaty of Imam Hasan (p) with

---

66. Bihar al-Anwar, al-Majlisi, Vol. 44, page 53

Muawiyah likely marked the beginning of the movement because it revealed the true nature and motives of the Umayyads. After the martyrdom of his brother in 50 AH, Imam Hussain (p) assumed the imamate and spiritual guidance of the people. For the next ten years, he busied himself with teaching the true religion of his grandfather, performing pilgrimage and even traveling to the outskirts of the Islamic nation. Muawiyah was aware that as long as Imam Hussain (p) was alive, he posed a threat to his kingdom, Moreover, he knew the sincere companions and followers of Ahl al-Bayt (p) would never give in and accept his tyranny. Thus, he ordered the execution of men like Hujr ibn Udi, who was one of the great companions of the Prophet and Imam Ali (p).[67] Upon hearing about the murder of Hujr ibn Udi, Imam Hussain (p) wrote a letter to Muawiyah protesting the crime and admonishing him against such injustice. He said, "Are you not the one who killed Hujr [and those with him]... unjustly out of aggression after you swore a strong oath and assured covenant that you would not punish them for what happened between you and them nor due to malice you had harbored against them?"[68] Other devoted companions who were unjustly killed by Muawiyah's agents included Rushayd al-Hajari, Amr ibn Hamaq, and Awfa ibn Haseen, and every time Imam Hussain (p) objected and spoke out.

---

67. al-Kamil, Ibn al-Athir, Vol. 3, page 468

68. Ikhtiyar ma'rifa al-rijal, al-Kashshi, page 99

Muawiyah died in 60 AH but not before he appointed his son Yazid as his successor. This was in direct violation of the treaty he had signed with Imam Hasan (p). Muawiyah wrote to Yazid from his deathbed, "I have constrained the challenges and warded off rebellion from you, and set up the matters [in your favor]. I have subdued the enemies, placed the reins of the Arabs in your hands, and accumulated for you what no one has ever done. I do not fear anyone opposing or fighting you for the caliphate except four men, Abdullah bin Umar, Abdullah bin Zubayr, Abdul Rahman bin Abu Bakr, and Hussain ibn Ali. Excessive worship has consumed Abdullah bin Umar, he will give in to you if left unaided. As for the son of Abu Bakr, he [only] follows what his companions pursue and his aspirations are only women and amusement. While the son of Zubayr is the one who lies in ambush like a lion, and he is the fox who is scheming and awaiting an opportunity to pounce upon you. If he revolts and you defeat him, separate every one of his joints. As for Hussain bin Ali, he is a high-minded person, and I hope that you will achieve revenge for our ancestors who were vanquished by his father and turned away by his brother. But the people of Iraq will not leave him until he is forced to rise up [alone]."[69] Furthermore, Muawiyah stopped at nothing to ensure the people accepted his son as the caliph, including bribery and threats.[70]

---

69. Tarikh al-Tabari, Vol. 5, page 323

70. Tarikh al-Kamil, Vol. 3, page 350; al-Bidaya wa al-Nihaya,

While Muawiyah was sly and shrewd, using the guise of piety as a cloak of deception, Yazid openly broke the tenets of Islam by drinking wine, promoting a court filled with singing, women, and debauchery.[71] Upon taking the caliphate from his father, he spread injustice and corruption in the society and spread fear among the people who did not agree with his policies. On the other hand, he knew that no amount of coercion would suffice his aspirations, and without the pledge of the tribal leaders and those of repute and respect among Muslims, his position would remain tenuous at best. Thus, Yazid sent his henchmen to secure the allegiance of various notable individuals across the Islamic nation, which clearly had to include the family of the Prophet. Zaynab (p) was with her brother Imam Hussain (p) in Madina when Yazid's emissaries came to Waleed ibn Utbah, who was Yazid's cousin and the governor of that city, instructing him to get the pledge from Imam Hussain (p) and other important men. Aware of what was transpiring, Imam Hussain (p) informed his family to be ready to respond to the Umayyad plot, and , went to meet Waleed ibn Utbah. When Imam Hussain (p) arrived at the meeting, another one of Yazid's cousins Marwan ibn Hakam, who was the former governor of the southwest Persian region of the Islamic nation under the third caliph Uthman and the governor of Madina under Muawiyah, was present to ensure there was no opportunity for

---

Vol. 8, page 31

71. *Ansāb al-ashrāf*, al-Baladhuri, Vol. 5, page 297

Imam Hussain (p) to walk away without giving his allegiance.

The order from Damascus was to secure Imam Hussain's allegiance at any cost, and to use lethal force in the event he resisted. Yet, they were no match for the wisdom and strategy of Imam Hussain (p), who used his highly-respected position in Madina to deflect the immediate demand for allegiance. Later when Marwan met Imam Hussain (p) on the street and advised him to give his allegiance to Yazid, Imam Hussain (p) responded, "Do you advise me to give allegiance to Yazid, who is an immoral man, away with you! We are the people of the household of the Messenger of God, truth is with us and it emanates from our tongues."[72] Shortly after, Imam Hussain (p) gathered Zaynab (p) and the other members of the family and instructed them to prepare for a hasty departure from Madina. Zaynab (p) must have anxiously awaited her brother as the two were never separated since birth. When she heard that he was getting ready to leave she took permission from her husband, who at the time was very sick and could not leave with them, and joined his caravan with Abdullah's two sons.

---

72. Maqtal al-Hussain, al-Khawarzimi, page 268

Chapter 4

·············•◆◆•·············

Zaynab (p) by the Side of her brother Hussain (p) from Madina to Karbala

Madina to Mecca

It is reported that Imam Hussain (p) visited the grave of his grandfather, mother, brother and other relatives[73] prior to departing Madina. He also wrote a will and testament to his brother Muhammad al-Hanafiyyah in which he unequivocally stated, "I did not march out in exultation, nor recklessly and without purpose, nor to seek corruption, and not to oppress anyone. Rather, I marched out seeking to reform my grandfather's nation. I want to enjoin what is right and forbid what is wrong and follow the sunnah of my grandfather and father 'Ali Ibn Abi Talib. So, whoever accepts that I am on the path of truth, [then] God is the Master of the truth, and whoever denies this, I shall persevere till God judges between me and the people;

---

73. Maqtal al-Hussain, al-Khawarzimi, page 269-270

surely He is the best of judges."[74] Hence, on the night of the 28th of Rajab, Imam Hussain (p) departed the city of his grandfather echoing the words of Prophet Musa (p) when he was leaving his home, "So he left the city afraid and cautious, saying, "Lord, protect me against the unjust people."[75]

Zaynab (p) started the journey of her life with her brother and their family. She became his unwavering support and a companion to him in every step they took. Upon leaving Madina, it must have been that she turned back and took one last look at the sanctuary her grandfather built, a place that would no longer feel the same. Yet, why did the ladies of the Prophet's family have to accompany Imam Hussain (p) on this journey, particularly given the political uncertainty and risk of harm? It must be that Imam Hussain (p) knew that not only could the daughters of the Prophet, especially Zaynab (p), face the calamities and trials that lay ahead, but that they would also persevere, and more importantly, become an essential voice of truth and defiance against tyranny and oppression. The stand of truthful, sincere, and pious women became an essential component of this resistance and continued the legacy started by Khadija (p) and Fatima (p).

---

74. Maqtal al-Hussain, al-Khawarzimi, page 273

75. The Holy Quran, 28:21

The carvan's journey from Madina to Mecca took about five days and upon beholding the sacred city Imam Hussain (p) recited the verse, "When he started his journey to Midian he said, "Perhaps my Lord will show me the right path."[76] As they entered Mecca, the news traveled quickly that the grandson of the Prophet was there. The people rushed to welcome and greet the family and asked Imam Hussain (p) the reason for his trip.

Imam Hussain (p) and the family of the Prophet remained in Mecca for the remainder of Shabaan, the month of Ramadan, Shawwal, and Dhil Qa'dah. During that time, Imam Hussain (p) met with several of the tribal elders and chiefs, including Abdullah ibn Umar and Abdullah ibn Abbas. Abdullah ibn Umar advised Imam Hussain (p) to enter into a treaty with Yazid out of fear that there would be a violent reprisal if he did not. Imam Hussain (p) responded to him, "How can I pledge allegiance to Yazid when the Messenger of God said what he did about him (i.e., his corruption, evil and deviousness)?" and then turned to Abdullah ibn Abbas and said, "Do you recognize that I am the son of the daughter of the Prophet?" To this Abdullah replies, "By God, yes! We do not know any other son of a daughter of a prophet other than you, and to support you is an obligation upon us like the obligation of fasting and paying alms-tax." Imam Hussain (p) says, "Then what

---

76. The Holy Quran, 28:22

do you say of a community of people who have expelled the son of the daughter of their prophet from his country and home, his birthplace, and the sanctuary of his grandfather?"[77]

This statement of Imam Hussain (p) also seems to reiterate the point that there were no other granddaughters of a prophet other than Zaynab (p) and Umm Kulthum. However, this did not concern those who were hell-bent on achieving their perverse objectives, nor did the sanctity of the holy household matter if they stood in their way. The news of Imam Hussain's stay in Mecca also reached beyond Hijaz to Kufah and Damascus. As such, the people of Kufah, many of whom were the supporters of his father and comprised the *shartatul khamees* or "Elite Guard" like Sulayman ibn Sard,[78] sent him letters of invitation and pledged to stand by him against the tyrant Yazid. Similarly, Imam received letters from the people of Basrah and possibly other regions. In the meantime, Imam Hussain (p) dispatched his cousin Muslim ibn Aqil to Kufah to confirm the reports and arrange the affairs in the event of their stand against the Umayyads. Muslim entered Kufah on the 25th of Shawwal and began to execute his cousin's directives.

---

77. Maqtal al-Hussain, al-Khawarzimi, page 278

78. The *shartatul khamees* or Elite Guard were a group of sincere believers who had pledged to support and defend Imam Ali

The days and weeks went by for the family of the Prophet in Mecca. For Zaynab (p), this was the place where her grandmother was revered and respected, and although the people recognized the special status of the Prophet's family, there was still a sense of apprehension towards them due to the prevailing political winds. With growing news of support in Iraq, it became increasingly clear that the grandson of the Prophet would depart Mecca and head there, particularly given he was informed that Yazid had sent Amru ibn Said ibn al-As with an army to lay siege upon Mecca, commandeer the pilgrimage and find and kill him at any cost.[79] Thus, in the early days of Dhil Hijjah, Imam Hussain (p) asked his family to prepare themselves to leave for Iraq. The people of Mecca begged him to stay, but Imam Hussain (p) was responding to the pledge of support from Kufah in order to stand up against Yazid and preserve Islam and the Islamic nation. Furthermore, he knew the consequence of remaining in Mecca. Imam Hussain (p) said to Abdullah ibn Zubayr, "I heard from my father that there is a ram that will be slaughtered in Mecca (i.e., in the sacred Mosque) and thereby violate its sanctity. I would prefer to be killed outside of Mecca, even if by a small span, than inside."[80]

---

79. Maqtal al-Hussain, Sayyid Abd al-Razzaq al-Muqarram, page 165

80. Maqtal al-Hussain, Sayyid Abd al-Razzaq al-Muqarram, page

On the 8th of Dhil Hijjah, as the pilgrims entered the sanctuary of the holy mosque and prepared for the pilgrimage, Imam Hussain (p), Zaynab (p), their family and close companions planned to depart Mecca. In their final hours there, Muhammad al-Hanafiyyah approached Imam Hussain (p) and said, "My brother, did you not promise me that you would consider the advice I gave to you (i.e., to remain in Madina, or instead, travel away towards Yemen)?" When Imam Hussain (p) answered, "Yes", Muhammad al-Hanafiyyah asked, "Then why are you departing so hurriedly [towards Iraq]?" Imam Hussain (p) said, "The Messenger of God came to me [in a dream] after I left you in Madina. He said to me, 'leave [your home], because God has decreed that you will be martyred." Hearing this Muhammad al-Hanafiyyah exclaimed, "Indeed we are from God and to Him is our return. Then what is the meaning behind taking the women [with you on this journey] when you are leaving under these circumstances?" Imam Hussain (p) replied, "[the Messenger said to me that] God has decreed [that they should be with me and] that they will be taken prisoners."[81]

In the same manner, Abdullah ibn Abbas said, "O' cousin, the people of Iraq are not to be trusted so do

---

166

81. al-Lahoof ala qatla al-tufoof, Sayyid ibn Tawoos, page 128

not go near them. Instead, stay here because you are the master of the people of Hijaz. If the people of Iraq truly want you then let them prove their loyalty by standing up to their enemy before you decide to go there." Imam Hussain (p) replied, "O' cousin, I know that you mean well with your advice but I have already decided to travel." Abdullah ibn Abbas then said, "If you are determined to go then leave behind your women and daughters because I fear that they will be killed if they are by your side." Imam Hussain (p) finally said, "By God, they (i.e., the Umayyads) will not stop [their assault] until they sever me from my root",[82] as if to say the ladies of the Prophet's family had no safe haven and that their destiny was alongside him. It is related that Zaynab (p) heard the conversation and immediately declared, "O' ibn Abbas, are you telling our master Hussain to leave us behind and travel alone [without us]. No by God! We came with him and we will leave with him, and we will die with him, and has the time left for us [any other divinely appointed guide] other than him?"[83] This was the unparalleled courage of Zaynab (p), who did not fear impending death, and more crucially, knew her role in supporting her brother in fulfilling his divine responsibility as the Imam.

---

82. Maqtal al-Hussain, Sayyid Abd al-Razzaq al-Muqarram, page 168

83. Madinat al-Maajiz, Sayyid Hashim al-Bahrani, vol 3, page 485

Mecca to Iraq

As the caravan prepared to leave Mecca, Imam Hussain (p) delivered a speech to those gathered, "All praise is to God, whatever He wills comes to pass and there is no power other than in Him, and may the peace and salutations of God be on His Messenger. Death is inscribed on the children of Adam like a necklace encircles a girl's neck. My desire to be reunited with my ancestors has never waned, just like Yaqub never stopped longing for Yusuf, and ordained for me is my demise which I shall soon meet. As if I see my limbs being torn apart by the wild beasts of the desert between al-Nawawis and Karbala, they will fill their empty bellies and insatiable innards through my death. The inevitable day decreed by the pen cannot be avoided. We the Ahl al-Bayt are satisfied with whatever satisfies God. We are patient in His trial and He will give us the reward of those who persevere. The Prophet's offspring shall never be separated from him, and they will be gathered by his side on the day all are in the presence of God. His eyes will be relieved to see them there and his promise to them will be fulfilled. Thus, anyone of you who is ready to sacrifice themselves in standing with us and is determined to meet God should accompany us because I will depart in the morning; God so wills."[84]

---

84. al-Lahoof ala qatla al-tufoof, Sayyid ibn Tawoos, page 126

After performing circumambulation of the Kaabah and performing the movements from Safa to Marwa on the 8th of Dhil Hijjah, Imam Hussain (p) gathered his sister, daughters and other kinfolk and departed from Mecca. Experiencing some resistance along the way, the caravan stopped at different places along the way from Mecca to Iraq. Throughout the journey, what must have been the state of Zaynab (p) as she saw her brother Hussain and other loved ones? At a few rest stops like al-Sifah and Dhat Irq, Imam Hussain (p) came across riders from Iraq, many of whom told him that the "hearts of the people of Iraq were with him but their swords were with the Umayyads".[85] In Khuzaymiyyah, which was almost half way between Mecca and Iraq, it is reported that Zaynab (p) came to speak to her brother the morning after they had settled in that place. She said, "My brother, can I tell you something that I heard yesterday?" Imam Hussain (p) replied, "What is that my sister?" She said, "I came out of the tent in the middle of the night for some need and I heard a voice saying, 'O eyes, celebrate with fervor! Who will mourn for the martyrs after me? Who will mourn those driven by fate of death? Destined to fulfill a sworn promise'" Imam Hussain (p) said to her, "O' my sister, whatever is decreed shall come to pass."[86] Such was the

---

85. Muthir al-Ahzan, ibn Nama, page 21

86. Maqtal al-Hussain, al-Khawarzimi, page 324

bond between brother and sister and their mutual dependence on God and their submission to His will.

After meeting Zuhair ibn al-Qayn in Zarud, the caravan advanced forward and stopped in Thalabiyyah during the afternoon, where Imam Hussain (p) fell asleep. He awoke with tears in his eyes and when his son Ali al-Akbar inquired about the cause he said, "My son, this is a time of the day when visions are never wrong. I saw in my dream that a rider approached me and said, 'O' Hussain, you are hurriedly advancing forward, and death is certainly hurrying you towards paradise.' It was then that I knew that our deaths had been announced to us." One wonders how these moments affected Zaynab (p), hearing her brother say those words and witness the resolve in him to continue his mission. There, she must have witnessed his response to the Kufan Aba Hurrah al-Azdi who asked him why he had left the sanctuary of God and the sanctuary of his grandfather in Madina with his women and children. He said, "O' Aba Hurrah, the Umayyads stole my wealth and I remained patient, they cursed my lineage and I [still] remained patient, they tried to spill my blood so I fled. By God, the rebellious aggressors will eventually kill me and then God will make them face complete humiliation and the sword of justice, and God will decree that they are overcome by those who trample on them...".[87]

Zaynab (p), her brother Imam Hussain (p), and their caravan passed through al-Shuquq and arrived at Zubalah. Here, they learned about the martyrdom of their cousin Muslim ibn Aqil at the hands of Ubaydallah ibn Ziyad.[88] The reports state that the entire caravan began to weep and mourn the loss of Muslim, and whereupon Imam Hussain (p) said, "May God have mercy upon Muslim, he has left this world and entered into God's relief, comfort and pleasure. He has fulfilled his destiny and now our destiny awaits us."[89] Could it be that among these travelers was a small girl who was anxiously awaiting news of her father during every step in the desert? Zaynab (p) would have brought her to her uncle Hussain (p) who would have sat her in his lap and consoled her for the loss of her father. This was only the beginning of the trials that lay ahead for Zaynab (p) and the other ladies. It is here that many people departed the company of Imam Hussain (p) having heard what happened to his emissary Muslim.

---

87. al-Lahoof ala qatla al-tufoof, Sayyid ibn Tawoos, page 131-132

88. Some historians state that Imam Hussain received the news of Abdullah ibn Yaqtur's (his other messenger to Kufah) martyrdom at Zubalah and that the news of Muslim ibn Aqil was received much earlier

89. al-Lahoof ala qatla al-tufoof, Sayyid ibn Tawoos, page 134

From there they traveled through Batn al-Aqabah until they reached Sharaf, where they encountered Hurr ibn Yazid al-Riyahi and his soldiers. True Islamic compassion and justice were shown by Imam Hussain (p) when he provided the enemy soldiers with water. Imam Hussain (p) stated to them that he had only arrived in that place because the people of Kufah had invited him with thousands of letters and had pledged their support to him. In response, Hurr declared that his orders were to escort Imam Hussain (p) and his followers to ibn Ziyad in Kufah and not allow him to deviate from this path in any way. It was then that Imam Hussain (p) ordered his women, children and companions to mount their rides and prepare to leave. The words of Imam Hussain (p) to his companions during this stage of the journey leave a lasting impression on us. He said, "The affairs as you behold have befallen us. The world has deceived and changed, its righteousness has faded and all that remains is corrupt and trivial. Do you not see that people do not act on the truth and they do not desist from evil? Truly the sincere believer seeks to be reunited with their Lord, and I see death as a happiness and continued life with the oppressors as only a humiliation."[90]

Imam Hussain (p), Zaynab (p), and their caravan kept moving in the desert. Every time they tried to change their direction they were forced back to the road that

---

90. al-Lahoof ala qatla al-tufoof, Sayyid ibn Tawoos, page 138

led to Kufah. This continued for all of them, women and children included, until they reached a place where Imam Hussain (p) asked, "What is this land called?" Five months and two days after leaving Madina, and approximately 24 days after leaving Mecca, they heard the name Karbala and stopped. Zaynab (p) heard her brother announce, "O' God, I seek refuge in you from the affliction (*karb*) and trial (*bala*), dismount [and set up the tents], it is here where our journey ends, where our blood will be spilled, and the place where our graves will be dug. This is also where our ladies will be taken prisoner, of this I have been told by my grandfather."[91] It was the 2nd of Muharram 61 A.H. and the trials of Zaynab (p) were about to begin, what lay ahead was a difficulty that she had been raised to face and in turn create an everlasting legacy for all of humankind.

---

91. Maqtal al-Hussain, al-Khawarzimi, page 337

Chapter 5

·············◆◆············

In Karbala

The Days Leading Up to Ashura

When the caravan left Qasr bani Maqatil, just before arriving in Karbala, Imam Hussain (p) was heard saying, "Surely, we belong to God and to Him we will return, and all praise belongs to God, Lord of the worlds". Ali al-Akbar was nearby, so he asked him why he kept repeating it. Imam Hussain (p) responded, "May God never permit you to see any evil." Ali al-Akbar then asked, "O' father, are we not on the path of truth?", to which his father said, "We are on the path of truth by the One to whom all the servants return." Ali al-Akbar proclaimed, "Then father, we are not afraid to die as long as we are right." Imam Hussain (p) said, "May God reward you with the best of what is given to a good son."[92] Those around the Imam sensed the immensity of what lay ahead of them. The tents were set up for Imam Hussain (p) and his family in Karbala, and those of his brothers and the children

---

92. al-Lahoof ala qatla al-tufoof, Sayyid ibn Tawoos, page 131

of his uncle around them. During that first night, Imam Hussain (p) sat in his tent and while fixing his sword recited, "O' time, woe upon you as a friend! How many do you have, at dawn and at dusk, of friends and of seekers of peril. While time is never satisfied with a substitute, but the affair is with the Most Mighty, and every living being will walk their path of destiny." It is reported that Ali al-Sajjad (p) said, "I heard my father repeating these lines several times, and I memorized them. I was choked with sorrow but I remained silent. However, when my aunt Zaynab (p) heard her brother, she could not bear out of her love for him and began to weep. She approached him and said, 'My brother Hussain, you are the light of my eyes. O' were death to have overtaken my life, you are the vicegerent of the past [divinely chosen ones] and the one the living turn to. This is talk from someone who is sure of being killed'. My father turned towards her and said, 'O' sister, seek solace in God, do not allow Satan to deprive you of your forbearance, for even the residents of the sky die, and the residents of the earth do not remain. Everything will perish except God, to Him belongs the rule and to Him will all return. So, where are my father and grandfather, who were both superior to me? They have tasted death and the dirt has consumed them. They were a righteous model for me and every believer.' He then consoled her and said, 'By my right upon you my sister, if I am killed, maintain your dignity in mourning me'".[93]

As the days passed, more soldiers descended upon Karbala with several thousands arriving with Umar ibn Saad and Shimr ibn Dhil Jawshan by the 6th of Muharram. Zaynab must have witnessed this accumulation of forces against her brother and seventy-two family members and companions. In the days that followed, the camp of Imam Hussain (p) was deprived of water and surrounded. Zaynab (p) knew that her brother Abbas would go to the river with a handful of companions to bring water for her, the other ladies, and the children. However, the water they received was sparse and the heat of the desert had taken its toll. The communications between Imam Hussain (p) and Umar ibn Saad did not benefit the latter in averting the crime that he had sought to commit. Imam Hussain (p) directed his companions to dig a trench on three sides of the camp to prevent a rear attack. With the enemy in front, Zaynab (p) heard her brother proclaim, "By God, take heed, do you know who I am?" They answered, "Yes! You are the son of the Prophet." Then, one by one he asked them, "By God, take heed, do you know that my grandfather is the Messenger of God? Do you know that my mother is Fatima daughter of Muhammad? Do you know that my father is Ali ibn Abi Talib? Do you know that my grandmother is Khadija bint Khuwaylid, the first lady

---

93. Maqtal al-Hussain, al-Khawarzimi, page 339

to accept Islam? Do you know that my uncle is Hamza, the master of the martyrs and uncle of my father? Do you know that Jafar al-Tayyar who is flying in Paradise with wings is my uncle? Do you know that the sword in my hand belonged to the Prophet? Do you know that this turban I am wearing belonged to the Prophet? Did you know that Ali was the first Muslim and the most knowledgeable of them and the most forebearing, and the master of every believer?" They all answered, "Yes!" Then she heard him ask, "Then why are you adamant about spilling my blood, when my father will be responsible for the pond in Paradise as the inhabitants of Paradise go to him like the camels flock to the water and the banner of honor will be in his hand?" They said, "We know all of this, but we will not desist until you are killed thirsty!"[94]

On the night of the 10th of Muharram, Zaynab (p) saw that her brother Hussain (p) had fallen asleep leaning on his sword as the enemy made preparations to attack. When he woke up she said to him, "My brother, the enemy is getting closer!" He told her that he saw their grandfather, mother, father and brother Hasan (p), who told him that he would be joining him shortly. Could Zaynab (p) have known that she would not be accompanying her brother when he was reunited with their grandfather? It was then that Imam Hussain (p) told Abbas (p) to relay to Umar ibn Saad that they should be given the night to pray and supplicate to God,

---

94. al-Lahoof ala qatla al-tufoof, Sayyid ibn Tawoos, page 147

and ask His forgiveness, because he loved prayer and recitation of God's book. Then, Imam Hussain (p) gathered his family and companions on the night before Ashura and after glorifying God he said, "Lord, I praise You for having taught us the Quran, given deep understanding about our religion, and honored us by making us the family of His Messenger, and bestowed upon us hearing, vision, and insight. Thus, make us of those who are grateful to You. I do not know any companions better than you, nor any family members more worthy or righteous than mine. May God reward all of you on my behalf. My grandfather, the Messenger of God, told me that I would go to Iraq and stop in a land called Karbala where I will be martyred. That time is upon me. The day of confronting these enemies will be tomorrow, so I give all of you permission to go freely. You are not obliged to stay with me from this moment forward. The darkness of the night has given you cover, so ride swiftly, and let each one of you take one man from my family with him. May God reward you all! Leave me with these people because they want no one other than me!"[95]

One by one, the family and companions declared, "O' son of the Messenger, what will the people say if we abandon you? What will we answer them? That we abandoned our chief and master, the son of the daughter of our Prophet, and that we didn't shoot an arrow or lift a sword to defend him or throw a spear

---

95. Tarikh al-Tabari, Vol. 6, pages 238-239; Maqtal al-Hussain, al-Khawarzimi, page 350

against his enemy? O' son of the Prophet, we will never abandon you, rather we will sacrifice ourselves for you and die in your defense." Zaynab (p) would have heard Muslim ibn Awsaja al-Asadi, Said ibn Abdullah al-Hanafi, Zuhair ibn al-Qayn al-Bajali, Burayr ibn Khudayr al-Hamadani, and other companions reaffirm their loyalty to her brother and declare their fearless stance next to him. History attests to the fact that many of the ladies of the families of these brave companions remained in Karbala with their men. Certainly the option to leave that place was afforded to them as it was to the companions of Imam Hussain (p). Yet, how could they leave when Zaynab (p) was still there? How could they abandon her knowing that what lay ahead was destitution, captivity and suffering? That night was spent in prayer and remembrance of God after the children were consoled and put to bed thirsty and bewildered.

The Day of Ashura

As the daybreak cut through the darkness of that long heavy night, a night Zaynab (p) must have spent collecting her strength. As the companions prepared to resist the enemies onslaught, Habib ibn Madhahir walked to the tents of the daughters of the Prophet, and standing outside declared, "O' honorable daughters of the Messenger of God! Before you are the swords of your slaves, who have vowed to never use them for anything except against those who wish to harm you!

Here are the spears of your slaves, who have sworn to lodge them in the chests of those who terrorize you!"

This day would mark history for generations to come as Imam Hussain (p) took a stand to preserve freedom and resist injustice and corruption. Imam Hussain (p) led the fajr prayers, and as the hours passed it became clear that the first assault of the enemy was near. The forces of Yazid had gathered in columns and were preparing to attack. Historians report that Imam Hussain (p) prayed to God upon seeing them, "My Lord, You are the one I trust in every difficulty, You are my hope in every hardship! You are my [only] trust and recourse during any affliction. How many worries cause the heart to be burdened, diminish the plans, cause the friend to betray, and elate the enemy, of these I complain [only] to You. I have placed my hope in You and no one else, and in turn, You removed and solved it. You are the source of every blessing and the ultimate fulfillment of every wish."[96]

As the anticipation of battle grew, Zaynab (p), who was in the camp, saw her brother advance towards the enemy and say, "O people! Listen to what I am about to say and do not rush [into what you are doing] until I admonish you with that which I owe you. Moreover, let me tell you why I have come here; thus, if you accept my explanation and believe me, and treat me with equity, you will be much happier and you will see there

---

96. Maqtal al-Hussain, Sayyid Abd al-Razzaq al-Muqarram, page 236; Tarikh Ibn 'Asakir, Vol. 4, page 233

is no reason to do what you are about to do to me."
Imam Hussain (p) continued advising the enemy
against their heinous actions and it stirred the
emotions and tears of the ladies in his camp. After
describing the human nature created by God and the
inevitable course that each person will be compelled to
follow, and the deception of the life of this world, he
said, "You declared obedience to the Messenger
Muhammad and belief in him, then you gathered
together to kill his progeny and offspring! Satan has
taken complete control of you and made you forget the
remembrance of God, the Great. Therefore, perdition
awaits you and will be your end. We belong to God and
to Him is our return. You are people who have turned
apostates after having believed, so away with the
oppressors. O' people, identify me, who am I? Then look
within and blame yourselves, and determine whether
it is permissible for you to violate my sanctity. Am I not
the son of your Prophet's daughter, the son of his
executor and cousin, the foremost to believe, and the
one who testified to the truth of what the Prophet
brought from his Lord?"[97] As the hearts of Zaynab (p)
and the other ladies were pained by these words, the
enemy remained unmoved. Finally, Imam Hussain (p)
declared to them, "Know that this illegitimate son of
the illegitimate father (i.e., Ubaydullah bin Ziyad) has
forced us to either unsheath our swords or succumb to
humiliation, and never will we accept humiliation!"

---

97. Maqtal al-Hussain, Sayyid Abd al-Razzaq al-Muqarram, page
237

Indeed, these words would echo in the demeanor, speech and resilience of Zaynab (p) in the days after Ashura. It is as if she carried the message of her brother that, "Surely God, His Prophet, and the sacred wombs [that have nursed us], which are modest and pure, refuse that we would ever bow down to those who are despicable, and they exhort us to exhaust every effort until we are killed. Beware, I shall fight you, even though many have deserted me and I only have a few men with me."[98]

Zuhayr ibn al-Qayn was assigned the commander of the right wing of Imam Hussain's army while Habib ibn Madhahir commanded the left wing and the standard was given to Abbas. They faced the enemy soldiers with their backs to the tents. Imam Hussain (p) directed them to fill the trenches with wood and light them on fire to deter the enemy from invading the camp. Having seen the tyranny of the enemy and their heartless actions, valiant and sincere men like Hurr repented and joined the side of Imam Hussain (p). It must have been the sounds of "Thirst! Thirst!" from the children in Imam Hussain's camp that moved their truthful hearts. Finally, Umar ibn Saad came forward and called upon all his soldiers to bear witness in front of the amir that he was the first to shoot an arrow at Imam Hussain (p). It was then that Imam Hussain (p) said to his companions and family members, "May God have mercy on you, stand and prepare to face death,

---

98. al-Lahoof ala qatla al-tufoof, Sayyid ibn Tawoos, page 156.

which is inevitable for all, the arrows being shot by these men are coming for you."

The battle started around the time of dhuhr prayers and in approximately two hours, Zaynab (p) saw that her brother Hussain had lost almost all his companions and his family. Each time one of them was mortally wounded he would call his master Hussain (p), "My final salutation upon you my master O' Aba Abdillah", who would charge the battlefield to bring the body back to the camp, many times having to pick up the shattered and cut pieces. These must have been the most heartbreaking moments for Zaynab (p) as she witnessed the martyrdom of companions like Muslim ibn Awsaja, Zuhair ibn al-Qayn, Habib ibn Madhahir, Burayr ibn Khudhayr, and Hurr ibn Yazid. Yet, more painful would have been what she saw happen to her family, especially the youths in the army of her brother. Which one of them had not been raised by Zaynab (p)? As the time of dhuhr prayer passed and all the companions had been martyred, one by one, the youths stepped forward to take the battlefield. In a short period of time, Zaynab (p) heard the calls of Ali al-Akbar, the one who resembled the Messenger of God, Qasim ibn Hasan, Abdullah ibn Muslim, Muhammad ibn Abdullah ibn Jafar, Jafar and Abdullah ibn Aqil, and her half-brothers Abdullah, Uthman and Jafar, who were the sons of Ali ibn Abi Talib from Fatima al-Kilabiyyah or Umm al-Baneen. Each one sent his final salutation as he fell from his horse and succumbed to his wounds. She even saw her son Aun ibn Abdullah ibn Jafar attack the enemy while reciting, "If you do not know me, I am the son of Jafar, the truthful martyr who lives in Paradise and flies with green colored wings, and this is enough of a testament on the day of Judgement." He was just a boy by today's standards, but certainly a mature and fearless soldier of God. How did Zaynab (p) the mother bear such a loss? It might be that she held him close during the farewell moment before battle and said to him, "My son, very soon you will be free and you will return to God a martyr. However, your mother will almost certainly be taken captive. Therefore, fight bravely in defense of your uncle Hussain, so that I may hold my head up high for your bravery and valor when I face the trials of captivity."

When all were martyred, Imam Hussain (p) dispatched Abbas (p) to bring water for the thirsty children. However, he was unable to fend off the enemy's attack, which descended upon him with spears, arrows and rods. He fell with severed arms and an arrow lodged in his eye. It was at this stage that Imam Hussain (p) expressed a sentiment that was likely not felt more deeply by anyone other than Zaynab (p). Upon seeing the body of Abbas, Imam Hussain said, "Now my back has broken and my strength has waned".[99] Abbas (p) was the standard-bearer of the army and the protector of the women and children, and moreover, the one who had provided for their every need during their journey. Zaynab (p) knew that her brother's time to go out and meet the enemy had come, but not before he sought

---

99. Bihar al-Anwar, al-Majlisi, Vol. 10, page 251

water for his son Abdullah, who was only six months old. Tragically, the innocent infant was met with an arrow from Harmala who killed him in his father's arms.

Now completely alone, Zaynab (p) must have heard her brother call from the hillock, "Is there anyone to support us? Is there anyone who will defend the sanctity of the Messenger of God's family? Is there any believer in the Unity of God who fears Him in safeguarding us? Is there anyone who will come to our rescue for the pleasure of God?"[100] Now the voices of the women could be heard crying even louder.

It is related that when Imam Hussain (p) made this call, the flap of one of the tents in his camp opened and his son Ali al-Sajjad (p) came out. He was very sick and leaning on a cane and dragging a sword saying, "I am coming father!" But, Imam Hussain (p) immediately beseeched Zaynab saying, "hold him back so that the world is not deprived of the progeny of Muhammad."[101] Such was the role of Zaynab (p) in protecting not only the progeny of her grandfather the Prophet, but also safeguarding the Imamate. She immediately took him back to the tent so no assault would fall upon him.

We cannot fathom the pain of those final moments for Zaynab (p). She was likely the one who helped him

---

100. al-Lahoof ala qatla al-tufoof, Sayyid ibn Tawoos, page 168

101. Tarikh al-Ya'qubi, vol. 2, page 217

dress for battle, giving him clothes that were not shabby and short so as to preserve his dignity. He also wore a simple piece of clothing underneath everything which he knew no one would be interested in stealing after his death. She then watched as he marched towards the battlefield and challenged the enemy soldiers one by one, vanquishing each one who came out to meet him. He charged against them and they fled from every one of his advances; he was after all the grandson of the Prophet and the son of the Commander of the Faithful. Zaynab (p) saw how they then attacked him from every side, showering the arrows down upon him. Zaynab's brother got down from his horse and called to the enemy, "O followers of Abu Sufyan, if indeed you have no religion, nor do you fear the return to your Lord, then at least be free in your life. Go back to your lineages and see if you are truly Arabs as you claim!" To this Shimr ibn Dhil Jawshan responded arrogantly, "What are you saying O' son of Fatima?" He said, "I am the one who is fighting you, and you are fighting me. However, the ladies have no role in this; so, keep your rogues away from them and stop them from attacking and harming the ladies of my family as long as I am alive."[102]

Zaynab (p) witnessed how her brother returned to the camp after fighting for some time. He came back to bid them a second farewell. Although Imam Hussain (p) directed this towards all the people in his camp, it

---

102. al-Lahoof ala qatla al-tufoof, Sayyid ibn Tawoos, page 168

seems his words may have been meant for Zaynab (p) in particular. He said, "Prepare yourselves for the trial, and know that God Almighty will protect and safeguard you, and He will save you from the evil of the enemies and make the ultimate end of your affair good. He will punish your enemy with various types of torture, and He will compensate you for this trial with many different types of comfort and honor. Therefore, do not complain, nor say anything that will demean you and lower your status." Zaynab's brother, the light of her eyes, the beloved of her heart, returned to the battlefield. No sooner did he resume attacking the enemy did she see that he was attacked from all sides. As he weakened, she saw him get struck with a rock on his head, which caused the blood to seep onto his beard. She watched as Harmala struck him with a three-pronged arrow in his chest. As the wounds and bleeding took their toll on her brother, standing at the door of the tent, Zaynab (p) witnessed the enemy strike him on his left shoulder and sever his arm while another struck him with an arrow in his mouth, and still another stabbed him in his chest. Zaynab (p) cried out, "O' Muhammad, O' father, O' Ali, O' Jafar, O' Hamzah. Behold Hussain slain in the open field of Karbala. Woe, had the skies fallen onto the earth. Woe, had the mountains crushed the valley." As he drew his last breaths, she shouted, "O' ibn Saad, will Abu Abdillah be killed while you look on?" Umar ibn Saad turned his face away from her. She demanded from all there, "Woe upon you, is there any [true] Muslim man among you?" It was finally the end she knew was coming, it was what her grandfather had promised would occur. In the heartbreaking tragedy of that moment, Zaynab watched as Shimr got down from his horse, kick her brother and sit on his chest, grab his beard and strike him several times with his sword before eventually severing his head.[103,104]

The Aftermath of Ashura

During the battle, Zaynab (p) comforted the women and children, and even gave solace to her brother Hussain. However, now there was no one left in the tents other than the women and children, and the living Imam Ali al-Sajjad (p), who had been too sick to fight in the battle. Zaynab (p) was given a great responsibility and the trust that was given to her is proof of the importance Islam gives to women in the preservation of its values and securing the future of society. This begs the question, if Islam is a religion that oppresses women and takes their rights away, how was it that the living imam placed its future in the hands of a woman?. But this was no ordinary task and Zaynab (p) was not an ordinary woman, she had been prepared for this through her upbringing and life's trials.

Only yesterday was she living in the house of prophethood surrounded by the love of her grandfather, but now she

---

103. Maqtal al-Hussain, al-Khawarzimi, Vol. 2, page 42

104. Read 'Who is Hussain' for complete details about the event of the day of Ashura

was alone and tyrannized by people who claimed to be his followers. Any other woman would not be blamed for collapsing after witnessing the brutal killing of her loved ones and the bloodshed of innocent men and youth.

It is reported that after Imam Hussain's martyrdom, his horse resisted capture by the enemy. Instead, he rubbed his mane in the blood of his deceased master and raced back to the tents where he began to neigh and hit the ground with his head as if to announce the tragedy that had befallen them to the people in the tents. When the daughters of the Prophet heard him, they began to weep and mourn.[105] Shortly thereafter, the enemy soldiers began looting the tents and setting fire to them. Nothing was spared, even the earrings were torn from the ears. The ladies began to flee in every direction as the heartless and evil soldiers showed no compassion or humanity towards them. There is a code of conduct and honor that one adheres to with their adversary, even in war; however, Yazid's forces reflected his immoral and lowly leadership during their ravenous plundering of the innocent women and children.[106]

Zaynab (p) now had to pick up the pieces and fulfill the trust that was placed in her. She gathered the women

---

105. Maqtal al-Hussain, al-Khawarzimi, Vol. 2, page 43

106. al-Kamil, Ibn al-Athir, Vol. 4, page 32; Tarikh al-Tabari, Vol. 6, page 260

and children who had run through the battlefield searching for the bodies of their loved ones. All the while, the ladies were being harassed and spears were thrown at them. It is reported that the wife of one of the enemy soldiers from the tribe of Bikr ibn Wail was present with him in the battlefield. She saw the ladies in that condition and taking a sword in her hand yelled out, "O' children of Bikr Ibn Wail, will you allow the daughters of the Messenger of God to be pillaged in this manner? There is no judgment except from God!" The outspoken woman was immediately ushered back to her tent by her husband.[107]

The bodies of the martyrs were also robbed of all possessions. How might Zaynab (p) have felt when the enemy soldiers took her brother's clothes, turban, sandals, and sword? She saw another soldier cut off his finger to steal his ring and then witnessed as they trampled his body under the horses' hooves until his chest was crushed to his back. Was this necessary after killing Imam Hussain (p)? These acts were meant to instill horror in the hearts of Zaynab (p) and the other survivors and humiliate them. However, the strength and honor of Zaynab (p) would overcome their lowliness. It is reported that the enemy descended upon the tent of Imam al-Sajjad (p), who was still lying on his mat in a state of severe illness. Although his life was spared at that moment, Zaynab (p) would have

---

107. al-Lahoof ala qatla al-tufoof, Sayyid ibn Tawoos, page 180

to protect and shield him during their prolonged captivity in Kufah and Damascus.

The heads of the martyrs were mounted on the tips of the spears and distributed among the tribal chiefs. The prisoners were tied up and marched through the battlefield between the bodies of their loved ones, which were left uncovered and unburied on the sands of Karbala. Each one of them began to weep and mourn when she saw her dead husband, brother or son. One of the observers of the events of Ashura relates, "By God, I will never forget Zaynab daughter of Ali [in that moment] when she saw the body of her brother Hussain and began to mourn and elegize him, "'O' Muhammad, may the angels of the sky send their salutations upon you, here is Hussain in the desert, he is covered with blood and his limbs have been cut off. Here are your daughters, they have been taken captive. Behold, your offspring have been slaughtered. To God is the complaint, and to Muhammad al-Mustafa, Ali al-Murtadha, Fatima al-Zahra, and Hamza master of the martyrs.'" Even among them was Sukaina, the young daughter of Imam Hussain (p), who clutched the body of her father until she was dragged off.[108] Zaynab (p) also saw the grief and pain on the face of her nephew Imam al-Sajjad (p), she said to him, "O' the legacy of my grandfather, father and brothers, why do I see you yearning for death? By God, this is what God revealed to your grandfather and father. God took a covenant

---

108. al-Lahoof ala qatla al-tufoof, Sayyid ibn Tawoos, page 180-181

from people who you do not know, the ones who have a status in this land and who are known to the residents of the heavens, that they will gather and bury these severed body parts and wounded corpses. Then they will erect a banner on this place for the grave of your father, who is the master of martyrs, the sign of which will never be destroyed, nor shall it ever be erased as long as there is day and night. Moreover, the promoters of apostasy and misguidance will try their best to destroy and efface it, instead, it shall only get more hallowed."[109] As they moved past the battlefield, Zaynab (p) raised her hands towards the sky and said, "O' God, accept from us this sacrifice." Imam Hussain (p) had fulfilled his covenant and now it was upon her to champion the religion of her grandfather.

---

109. Kamil al-Ziyarat, ibn Qawlawayh, page 361

Chapter 6

·············●◆●·············

The Captives in Kufah

There were approximately 20 women and children who were chained and forced to ride on camels without saddles. The soldiers whipped them if they cried or became too weak to travel. Zaynab (p) embraced the children and held them close to protect them from the whips. After a journey that took about two days, they were on the outskirts of Kufah where the people had gathered to look at them. It is related that a Kufan woman approached the captives and asked who they were, the ladies answered, "We are captives from the family of Muhammad!" When the woman heard this response, she immediately brought veils for them to cover themselves with. Seeing this sight and shocked at their state the people who had gathered began to weep and express their sorrow.

Ibn Ziyad ordered his soldiers to parade the captives through the streets as they were brought to his court. The bystanders felt pity and started to bring them dates and water. It was then that Umm Kulthum, the younger sister of Zaynab (p), declared, "O' people of Kufah, charity (sadaqah) is forbidden upon us the family of the Prophet"[110] All of a sudden, the weight of the heinous crime that had been committed began to dawn on them. They had invited her brother and pledged to him their support, and it was their betrayal that led to the tragedy of Karbala.

Then, Zaynab (p) delivered an eloquent speech that shook the people to their cores as they listened in shame for the part they played in the killing of the only grandson of the Prophet of Islam. When it appeared that she was about to speak, the people suddenly became quiet, everyone was attentive and even the bells of their animals stopped ringing. Zaynab (p) began by praising God, then she sent salutations on the Messenger, but she referred to him not as *Rasulallah* or *al-Nabi*, but rather as "my grandfather Muhammad".[73] It was in that moment that she ignited the hearts of the listeners as they suddenly became aware of who she was and what she represented to Islam and all Muslims. After all, none of them could claim such a kinship to the Prophet and indeed Zaynab's words reflected the prominent position of the Ahl al-Bayt (p) from the Holy Quran. Some may have even suddenly recognized her as soon as she made this statement because of her previous residence in Kufah during the caliphate of her father.

It is reported that Bashir ibn Khazim al-Asadi said, "On that day, I looked upon Zaynab daughter of Ali and I did not see a more dignified lady with an eloquence that

---

110. al-Lahoof ala qatla al-tufoof, Sayyid ibn Tawoos, page 192

conjured the memory of the Commander of the Faithful Ali. [And with her gripping presence] She gestured to the people to be silent."[111] The daughter of Ali and Fatima boldly spoke, "O people of Kufa, you are people of deception and treachery, why do you now cry?! Spare your [false] tears and restrain your feigned cries, your example is that of 'the lady behind the spinning wheel who has broken the yarn by pulling it with unnecessary force, and you must not consider your oaths as means of deceit".[112] Zaynab's unparalleled knowledge of the Holy Quran was apparent for all to behold as she challenged the people to consider how they had sworn to uphold the Book of God and the sunnah of His Prophet and subsequently undone their oaths. This is a timeless message of the Aqeela Zaynab (p) who reminds us today that our oath to God and His Prophet is not compromisable nor of calculable value such that it can be bought or sold or used to derive personal benefit.

Zaynab (p) continued, "Is there anyone among you who is not arrogant in [worldy] possession, lecherous, deceitful and two-faced, bearing an unjustified grudge, a meek bondmaid, an agitator, fertile for the prejudicial, or an indicator of that which is of no use and buried? Vile is what your souls have incurred, you have invoked the wrath of God upon yourselves and you will remain in the chastisement for eternity." The

---

111. al-Amali, Shaykh al-Mufid, page 321

112. The Holy Quran, 16:92

effect of her eloquent language and the use of pointed terminology, both in direct accusation and subtle inference, could only come from someone who was raised under the care and direction of God's appointed personalities. This was a knowledge and skill not acquired in a school or university, but rather imparted through divine culture and a purified lifestyle. It points to the importance of learning, personal enrichment and value that Islam gives to women, and clearly shows that it is available to everyone.

She asked, "Do you [now] really weep and lament? By God, you should weep incessantly and barely laugh because you have brought upon yourselves nothing but shame and ignominy, and you shall never be rid of its tarnish no matter how many times you try to cleanse yourselves!" In this part of her speech, Zaynab (p) reminded the people that there are certain evils that when committed could not be atoned for because their consequences were so dire that the negative impact was beyond the individual sinner. "You will never be absolved of, nor wash away, the killing of the descendant of the seal of messengers, the essence of the message [of God], the master of the youths of Paradise, the refuge of the best amongst you, the aversion of calamity from you, the lantern of your proof [in front of God], and the one who is in charge of your affairs. O' how horrible a burden you bear! You are wretched [in the eyes of God], may you be crushed. Your effort is futile, your toiling has come to nothing, you have squandered your opportunity, and you have earned nothing but the wrath of God and His

Messenger. And, you will be doomed with humiliation and destitution." She was not deterred by death, nor afraid, to point out the gravity of their actions. The killing of the Imam of the time was a crime against humanity and an unforgivable violation of God's sacred religion. Moreover, she put into clear perspective that nothing would avail them despite having the worldly possessions and apparent power in the land. It was Zaynab's way of awakening the people's consciences so that there would be no excuse that the truth was not known.

"Woe upon you, O' people of Kufah! Do you even know that you assaulted and crushed a part of the Messenger of God's body? Do you even know which of his most beloved possessions you have defiled, which of his blood you have shed, and which of his sanctity you have violated? What a shrewd and emboldened feat and horrific deed you have achieved. Are you surprised that the skies rained blood [as a result of what you have done]? Verily the punishment of the next world is a greater chastisement and there will be no one to help you. Therefore, do not be deceived by the respite [given to you], because haste will not speed it up, nor is there any risk that its opportunity for revenge will be lost. Your Lord keeps an eye on all [evil-doing people]." It was not until her nephew requested her to stop that she ended her speech. He further said, "Praise is to God, [my aunt is] a learned lady whom no one has taught, one who understands without needing anyone to explain to her."[113] As the people of Kufah considered Zaynab's final words, the sanctity of God's symbols must have become apparent and the focus of their attention. God says, "To respect the symbols of God is the sign of a pious heart"[114] and she bluntly pointed out that her brother Hussain-(p) was one of those signs. Today, she perpetually reminds us that the preservation of these symbols, in particular the legacy of her brother, is the key to holding on to our Islamic identity and ensuring it remains unblemished generation after generation.

Imam al-Sajjad (p), Umm Kulthum and Fatimah daughter of Hussain, all spoke to the Kufan crowd with Zaynab (p). Yazid's men thought that by killing Imam Hussain (p) they had silenced the family of the Prophet, and more importantly, made an example of them in front of the Islamic nation. Yet, they stood with so much strength, resilience and fearlessness, especially the sister of Hussain. She shook the ground under their feet with her speech, which became a defiance against tyranny and injustice for all time. This was a speech that sought to hold people accountable for their actions and awaken them from their heedlessness. Zaynab (p) taught the people of Kufah a very valuable lesson, that the most powerful weapon is the truth. It is clear Imam Hussain (p) did not bring Zaynab (p) with him aimlessly,

---

113. al-Ihtijaj, al-Tabarsi, page 166

114. The Holy Quran, 22:32

she had an important role to play in carrying on her brother's mission.

The army led the captives to the governor's court where ibn Ziyad was sitting on his throne. The head of Imam Hussain (p) was brought in and placed in front of him. He kept striking the mouth of Zaynab's brother with a stick, the same mouth that was kissed by the Prophet. The court was filled with people and the captives were huddled in a corner with Zaynab (p) disguised among them. Yet the mark of the Prophet's family could not be hidden because very soon after entering the court, ibn Ziyad noticed a dignified lady and asked about her. He was told that she was Zaynab, daughter of Ali. As soon as he learned her identity, he turned towards her and said, "Praise be to God who shamed you and proved you to be liars." Zaynab replied, "Praise be to God who honored us through His Prophet and cleansed us from all filth. Verily the transgressor is humiliated and the deviants lie and we are neither of those."[115]

Agitated, ibn Ziyad retorted, "How do you feel about what you witnessed happen to your brother and your family?" In that moment, the daughter of Fatima gave a reply that only one who is deeply connected and dependent on her Lord could give, she said, "I have only witnessed beauty! These are people whom God has chosen to fight [in His way and be martyred], and they hastened to fulfill His call. Moreover, God will gather

---

115. al-Lahoof ala qatla al-tufoof, Sayyid ibn Tawoos, page 201

you up [after death] and you will be held responsible for what you have done. You will [then] witness who will be the victor on that day. May your mother mourn you O' son of Marjanah!" Ibn Ziyad became enraged by her boldness and courage, and he moved to attack her but was reminded by someone that she was only a woman, and the word of a woman should never be taken seriously.[116] Thus, hoping that his words would provoke her to lose her poise, he continued saying, "God has healed my heart by neutralizing your tyrant [brother] Hussain and the rebels from his family." However, Zaynab (p) would not crumble or compromise her dignity, she immediately responded, "By my life! You have killed my protector, persecuted my family, cut off the branch of my family and pulled out my roots. So, if this heals your heart, then you are certainly healed."

When ibn Ziyad realized that he was not about to break the daughter of Ali (p) and Fatima (p), he turned his aggression on her nephew Ali al-Sajjad (p), who was still suffering from illness. Having failed to instigate Imam al-Sajjad (p) and grown even more aggravated, ibn Ziyad ordered the guards to execute him. No sooner had the order been given that Zaynab (p) stepped in front of her nephew and said, "O Ibn Ziyad, you have not left any of us alive, if you want to kill him, then kill me with him as well." Then Imam al-Sajjad (p) added, "Don't you know that we are accustomed to being

---

116. al-Lahoof ala qatla al-tufoof, Sayyid ibn Tawoos, page 201

killed and that martyrdom is one of God's blessings upon us?"[117] Frustrated and unable to respond, ibn Ziyad ordered for the captives to be imprisoned in a house opposite the mosque.

Despite being imprisoned, the impact of Zaynab's words were profound. People began to express their resentment for what had happened, and they gathered at the door of their prison wailing and beating their faces.[118] However, Zaynab (p) shouted at them, "None of the women of the Arabs have any right to visit us [in this state]. Only the maidservant and bond woman may visit us because they have endured captivity and difficulty like us."[119] Not long after, ibn Ziyad wrote to Yazid informing him that Imam Hussain (p) had been killed and that his family were being held prisoners. Yazid responded and ordered him to send the heads of Imam Hussain (p) and the martyrs as well as the captives to Damascus.

On the Way to Damascus

The calamity that befell the women and children in Damascus has broken hearts for centuries. Imagine that you have a young daughter who is torn away from her home and made to endure trials that a grown

---

117. al-Lahoof ala qatla al-tufoof, Sayyid ibn Tawoos, page 202

118. Rawdat al-Wa'idhin, al-Naishapuri, page 163.

119. al-Lahoof ala qatla al-tufoof, Sayyid ibn Tawoos, page 202

person could not withstand, or a sister who is subjected to untold cruelties and torture. This was the continuing pain of the family of the Prophet after the events of Karbala. The heads of Imam Hussain (p) and the other martyrs were mounted on the spears and carried ahead of the women and children as they were made to travel from Kufah to Damascus. It is reported that Imam al-Sajjad's hands were tied and fastened to his neck while the women were similarly tied together. Although there was a direct route from Kufah to Damascus, Yazid's evil soldiers took the captives via a longer and more treacherous route in order to parade them in front of the residents of various towns and villages. During the journey, the women and children would become exhausted and at times fainted from dehydration. It is reported that some of the captives may have even perished during the journey and Imam al-Sajjad (p) buried them on the way with the help of his aunt Zaynab (p). Despite the fact that Yazid wanted to show people his might and his so-called defeat of the family of the Prophet, which he envisioned would instill terror in the hearts of people and subservience, the reaction was the opposite. Residents of many places between Kufah and Damascus witnessed the ugliness and evil of what he and his men had done, and instead, marveled at the forbearance and resistance of the family of the Prophet, especially the daughters of the Messenger. It became clear to them that the valor they were witnessing in Zaynab (p) and the other captives was a result of something invaluable that needed to be protected at all costs.

As the captives neared Damascus, Umm Kulthum said to Shimr ibn Dhil Jawshan, "I have a request from you." He said, "What do you want?" She said, "If you take us into the city, then I request that you do so on a road that does not have a lot of people (i.e., so there won't be spectators)? Also, tell your soldiers who are carrying the heads to travel some distance ahead of us so any spectators will become engrossed with looking at them and not the daughters of the Prophet." Instead, Shimr ordered that they be taken on the busiest road and he instructed the men carrying the heads to ride in the middle of the ladies so all the spectators would stare at them while simultaneously looking at the heads.[120] They were then brought to the main entrance of the city and forced to stand there for a period, which was how slaves and prisoners were dealt with in Damascus.

---

120. al-Lahoof ala qatla al-tufoof, Sayyid ibn Tawoos, page 210

Chapter 7

············◆◆◆············

Captives in Damascus

Zaynab and the other captives entered Damascus on the 1st of Safar with the residents cheering, beating drums and celebrating as if the city was holding a festival. It is clear that the people were told that a great victory had been achieved over a group of rebels and that the nation was secured from their trouble. Men, women and children came out wearing the best of their clothing, they decorated the streets and held up colorful banners. This propaganda was the modus operandi of Muawiyah, who would use misinformation to control the masses and manipulate the machinery of government to his advantage. The people of Damascus were under the impression that they had just defeated an enemy of Islam and that the brave defenders of freedom were bringing captive women from a foreign enemy. As the captives were made to walk through the city, the residents started jeering them and hurling insults. It is reported that an old man came close to the ladies of Imam Hussain's family and said, "Praise be to God that you were killed and you perished, and by doing so relieved the people from you and enabled the commander of the faithful to defeat you."[121] Imam al-Sajjad (p) asked him, "O' shaykh, have you read the Holy Quran?" The old man replied, "Yes", then Imam al-Sajjad (p) asked him, "Do you know this verse, 'I do not ask you for any payment for my preaching to you except [your] love of [my near] relatives'?"[122] The old man answered, "I have read that verse." Imam al-Sajjad (p) then said, "We are the relatives, O' shaykh." Imam al-Sajjad (p) asked him, "Have you also read the following verse, 'People of the house, God wants to remove all kinds of uncleanliness from you and to purify you thoroughly'?"[123] The old man responded, "Yes, I have read that verse." Then Imam al-Sajjad (p) declared, "We are the people of the house, O' shaykh!" The old man was shocked and became silent with guilt, then he asked, "Are you really them?" Imam al-Sajjad (p) replied, "We are them by the right of our grandfather the Messenger of God." The old man began to weep profusely as he lamented the killing of the family of the holy Prophet. He announced, "Let God witness that I dissociate myself from the ones who killed you." He repented for his behavior and sought forgiveness at the hands of Imam al-Sajjad (p). Unfortunately, the news of this elderly man's reformation reached Yazid who immediately ordered him to be killed.[124]

---

121. al-Lahoof ala qatla al-tufoof, Sayyid ibn Tawoos, page 211

122. The Holy Quran, 42:23

123. The Holy Quran, 33:33

124. Maqtal al-Hussain, al-Khawarzimi, Vol. 2, page 61

The captives were tied with ropes before being paraded into the court of Yazid. Zaynab (p) and Umm Kulthum were tied together around their necks and then to Imam al-Sajjad (p). When they finally came face to face with the tyrant, Imam al-Sajjad (p) said, "How do you think the Messenger of God would react if he could see us in this state?" The murmurs began to rise in the crowd, so Yazid ordered the ropes to be released. Sitting on his throne, Yazid ordered for the head of Imam Hussain (p) to be brought and placed in front of him. It is related that when the eyes of Zaynab (p) fell upon her brother's head, she began to weep and say, "O' Hussain, O' the beloved of the Messenger of God, O' the son of Mecca and Mina, O' the son of Fatima al-Zahra the master of all ladies, O' the son of the daughter of Mustafa."[125] The daughter of Fatima made everyone cry while Yazid remained silent and emotionless.

Instead, Yazid turned towards Imam al-Sajjad (p) and said, "How do you see what was done to your father Hussain?" He answered, "I see only that which God, the Most Exalted, has decreed before creating the heavens and the earth!" Yazid retorted, "Whatever hardship befalls you is the result of your own deeds"[126] as if to demean Imam al-Sajjad (p), the chosen deputy of God, and insinuate the reason they were in such a condition. Imam al-Sajjad (p) replied, "This verse was not revealed

---

125. al-Lahoof ala qatla al-tufoof, Sayyid ibn Tawoos, page 213

126. The Holy Quran, 42:30

in reference to us, instead, the verse about us is, 'Whatever hardships you face on earth and in your souls were written in the Book before the creation of the souls. This is certainly easy for God. so that you would not grieve over what you have lost nor become too happy about what God has granted to you'.[127] Therefore, we do not grieve over what we have lost nor feel elated about what we have gained." Knowing that he did not even possess a small measure of Imam al-Sajjad's knowledge, Yazid began to recite poetry in response, which is when the former asked that he be allowed to speak. Although Yazid was hesitant to give him permission, he begrudgingly acquiesced because the people gathered there insisted upon hearing him. It is reported that Imam al-Sajjad (p) delivered a speech that shook the hearts of the people and brought tears to their eyes.[128] Imam warned the people about the life of this world and the delusion of seeking its ornaments. So that there would be no doubt, he declared to them who he was and who his ancestors were, beginning with the Prophet, and then taking the names of Lady Khadija (p), Imam Ali (p), Lady Fatima (p), Hamza and others. He continued to describe their unparalleled status in the eyes of God and in the service of Islam, and their extraordinary qualities until fearful of discord, Yazid yelled at the caller to recite the call to prayer.

---

127. The Holy Quran, 57:22-23

128. For the full text of Imam al-Sajjad's speech, read Maqtal al-Hussain by Sayyid Abd al-Razzaq al-Muqarram, Maqtal al-Hussain by al-Khawarzimi or one of the other authentic historical accounts of this tragedy

However, the impact of his speech was palpable and the people's consciences began to question the lies they had been told.

In that court, Zaynab (p) continued to play the role of the family's protector. While there, a Syrian man stepped forward and asked Yazid to give him Fatima, the daughter of Hussain, as a servant. The young child clutched onto her aunt Zaynab (p) and said, "My aunt, how could this happen that I will serve him?" Zaynab replied, "This will never happen as long as I am here!" Hearing this, Yazid said, "I will make this happen if I so choose." Then Zaynab (p) answered defiantly, "It is not possible unless you turn from your religion." Yazid said, "Your father and brother are the ones who turned from the religion." So Zaynab (p) said, "By the religion of God and the religion of my grandfather I swear that it was through my father and brother that you and your father were guided [to the right way] if you had been a Muslim at all!" Yazid said to her, "Enemy of God, you lie!" She spoke in a pointed tone, "You are a [so-called] leader over people's destinies; yet, you taunt and oppress others." It was Zaynab's intention to hold Yazid accountable in front of the gathered crowd and present the proofs of God so that no one would dispute the truth. It was then that the Syrian man repeated his request to take Fatima (p), but this time Yazid rejected it outright and scolded him saying, "May God give you that which results in your end!"[129] Sadly, the tragedies

---

129. Tarikh al-Tabari, Vol. 6, page 265; Ibn al-Athir, Vol. 4, page 35

continued on the daughters of Imam Hussain (p) despite this crime being averted. Although the identity is not entirely agreed upon by historians and scholars, various reports indicate that a four year old daughter of Imam Hussain, either Sukaina or Ruqayyah, died in the prison of Damascus and was buried there during captivity. Today, her shrine there serves as a reminder of the blind cruelty of Yazid and the price paid by the family of the Prophet to preserve Islam and human dignity.

Zaynab (p) took a stand for all of humanity in the courtyard of Yazid, she spoke resonating the words of her mother Fatima (p). Zaynab (p) began by extoling God saying, "All praise to God, Lord of the worlds, and may His peace and blessings be upon Muhammad and his family. Truly God is truthful when He said, 'The end of the evil-doers was terrible, for they had rejected the revelations of God and mocked them.'[130] O' Yazid, do you assume that when you constricted upon us the roads and horizons of the sky that we became slaves or captives, and as such, that we were [somehow] forsaken by God and you were honored? And that what has occurred [to us] is because you have a great status with Him? Thus, you are boasting about your [so-called] greatness and arrogantly looking down on us? You are elated and pleased because you perceive the world is submitting to you, the conditions are as you wanted, and you consider that our status and authority has become yours? But, wait and be aware, have you

---

130. The Holy Quran, 30:10

forgotten what God has said, 'The unbelievers must not think that Our respite is for their good. We only give them time to let them increase their sins. For them there will be a humiliating torment'[131]." Zaynab (p) points that what may be perceived in the life of this world to be success and achievement can oftentimes turn out to be a noose around one's neck when God's judgement arrives. Thus, she reminded not only Yazid and his evil followers, but also all people that true success can only be measured by piety and service as determined by God. Zaynab's opening, and indeed her entire speech in Damascus which is likely unparalleled by any other woman in history, shines a light on today's oppressors and those who believe that they are impervious to justice because they have achieved a measure of worldly gain.

Zaynab (p) continued fearlessly, "O' illegitimate son, what type of justice is it that you veil and safeguard your bond women and wives in your private chambers while at the same time you parade the daughters of the Messenger of God as captives. Indeed, you have forced them to come out of their dwelling of modesty and chastity, allowed them to be in plain view for all to see, and permitted the enemy to drag them from one place to another so that they may be seen at every oasis and garrison. Their faces are exposed for people to see from far and wide, by the lowly and honorable, while they have none of their male guardians or protectors."

---

131. The Holy Quran, 3:178

Zaynab (p) emphasized the chastity of the women of the household of the Prophet, and moreover, showed that what Yazid had committed was a crime no one had done before. Irrespective of considering their status, he did not adhere to any code of battle in which the women and children of an enemy should not be harmed. This was the code of Islam and Yazid had violated it in every aspect.

She said, referring to Yazid's grandmother Hind, and comparing his lowly lineage to her honored and lofty one, "Yet, what can be expected from the descendants of those whose mouths chewed the liver of the purified people and who benefitted from the blood of the martyrs? How can the one who glances at us with hatred, malice and animosity bask in our [the Ahl al-Bayt] oppression? Moreover, you recite [and celebrate] without any feeling of guilt or conscience, 'They will laud and say in elation, O' Yazid, may your hands never be paralyzed!'" Here, Zaynab (p) points out to him that the celebrations and praise of victory does not erase the generations of corruption and evil that was so deeply rooted in Yazid's family.

Yazid tried to instigate, provoke and pain Zaynab (p) and the other captives. He kept striking the head of her brother, which was placed like a trophy in front of him. She declared, "You strike the lips of Abu Abdillah, how dare you! He is the master of the youth of Paradise. You have unwrapped a wound that was almost healed, and why would you not do so, and shed the blood of the progeny of Muhammad and the celestial beings from the family of Abd al-Mutallib, when there is no mercy in your heart? And, you simultaneously call upon your ancestors [to bear witness to this crime] as if you are actually speaking to them. You will be in the same place as them very soon, and you will wish that you were actually paralyzed and silenced so that you could never do and say what you did."

In front of all who were present, Zaynab invoked, "O' God, restitute our rights that were taken away from us, seek revenge against those who oppressed us, and unleash Your wrath against those who spilled our blood and killed our protectors. [O' Yazid] You have only burned your own skin and torn your own flesh, and you will face the Messenger of God bearing the responsibility of having shed the blood of his progeny, violating his sanctity and the sanctity of his women and family, and his flesh and blood. Surely, God will gather them together and will demand justice for them, 'Do not think of those slain for the cause of God as dead. They are alive with their Lord and receive sustenance from Him.[132]" This was an important statement by Zaynab (p) because although Yazid was not present in Karbala or Kufah, he was the direct instigator and perpetrator of the crime. She emphasized that it is not only the person who directly commits the crime who is culpable; instead, those who order it, support it, and lend it their silent acceptance are also guilty.

132.The Holy Quran, 3:169

She declared, "God is sufficient as the judge over you, Muhammad will be your antagonist, and Archangel Jibrail will be your foe. How perilous will be the end of the oppressors, those who enable you to do what you did after having given you charge over the Muslims? Which of you will have the more severe outcome and will be the most exposed [to God's wrath]?" What foresight from the granddaughter of the Prophet, who in speaking these words to Yazid taught us about being responsible in appointing our leaders and those we support to run society.

Pointing to the state of affairs and her own need to speak out against what was happening, she said, "Despite the fact that this tragedy has forced me to have to speak to you, I still consider you to be small (i.e., lowly), your insults to be greatly vile, and your rebuke to immense, but these eyes are tearful and the chests are filled with sorrow [from the tragedy we have experienced]." Even though her strength and resilience were immeasurable, Zaynab (p) wanted to show to the people that what was done to them was a profound loss and had caused them great pain. She continued, "It is the most peculiar thing that the honored party of God is killed by the disavowed army of Satan. Their hands are drenched in our blood and their mouths contain our flesh, while those pure bodies are being devoured and violated by the wild beasts of the desert. If you think that we are a prize for your victory, you will soon find out the consequences of what you have done because surely your Lord never does injustice to His servants. Therefore, all complaints are to God and upon Him do we depend."

In the last part of her speech, Zaynab (p) boldly states that no matter what Yazid does, he will never truly succeed. Even though it appears that injustice and oppression have triumphed in the life of this world, truth and justice will eventually prevail because this is the promise of God. She says, "So plot whatever schemes you have and expend as much effort as you want [in achieving them], [but remember] by God, you will never erase the memory of us, eradicate our inspiration, reach our status nor rid yourself of this shame." Has the memory not remained, and even grown, since those fateful days? Who is remembered, lauded, and cherished? History and current circumstances attest to the fact that Zaynab words were true and profoundly poignant about the legacy of her brother and what he achieved. On the other hand, she proved to Yazid, "Your view will be futile, your days will be short, and your wealth will not avail you on the day when the caller announces, 'may the curse of God be on the oppressors'. Praise to God who sealed the life of our early ancestors with happiness and forgiveness, and for our last ones with martyrdom and mercy. We ask God to complete His reward for them and increase His bestowal upon them, and make our succession successful and good. He is

Most Merciful and Most Compassionate, and God is sufficient for us and the best advocate."[133]

Zaynab (p) shook the walls of Yazid's illegitimate foundation with these powerful words. He could do nothing but hang his head in embarrassment having been outclassed by the granddaughter of the Prophet. Having no other recourse, he ordered them to be removed from his presence immediately. He would later resort to feeble and inhuman attempts to torture the captives. He could not defeat Zaynab (p) and the family with words or any other reasonable means, so instead, he chose to employ cruel tactics in an attempt to break their spirit. He instructed his soldiers to hang the head of Imam Hussain (p) above the door to his court. He would then order Imam al-Sajjad (p) and the women and children to come to the court so that they would be forced to see the head of their beloved Hussain (p). It is reported that the women would enter weeping and mourning after having been reminded of their loss.[134] Such was the heartlessness and evil of Yazid, who ordered that the captives be held in a rundown house that did not provide them any shelter from the sun or heat.

133. al-Lahoof ala qatla al-tufoof, Sayyid ibn Tawoos, page 217-218

134. Maqtal al-Hussain, al-Khawarzimi, Vol. 2, page 81

Chapter 8

·············•◆•·············

Return to Karbala

The days spent in Damascus were immensely difficult for the family of the Prophet. One day, the guards allowed Imam al-Sajjad (p) to come out of the prison and walk outside on the streets. A man approached him and asked, "How are you this evening, O' son of the Messenger of God?" Imam al-Sajjad (p) replied, "We have received the evening like the Israelites did when they were among the people of Pharaoh, who killed their sons and took their women captive. The Arabs boast to the non-Arabs that Muhammad was one of them, while Quraish boasts to the rest of the Arabs that Muhammad was of them. We the family of the Prophet [who are both Arab and Quraishi, and moreover, the progeny of the Prophet] are now destitute; thus, [all we can say is] to God we belong, and to Him shall we all return." The man later recounted, "While he was talking to me, a woman came out after him [hurriedly] and called, 'Where are you going, O' best of successors [of my grandfather, father and brother]?' He quickly left me and went back to her. I inquired about that woman's identity, and I was told that she was his aunt Zaynab."[135]

Yazid allowed Zaynab (p) and the family of Imam Hussain (p) to mourn him and recall his martyrdom, thus began the tradition of majlis al-Hussain as practiced by her. Although they continued to mourn for several days, their desire was to leave that hostile city and return to their home. In any case, the speech of Zaynab (p) and the stand of the holy progeny against Yazid's despotism and corruption stimulated a tide of change. Moreover, the profoundness of her strength and resilience, of a woman boldly speaking out with wisdom and eloquence in a predominantly patriarchal society, had an awakening effect on those who had dismissed them as weak and unable to lead a movement of change and reformation. As such, Yazid realized that he risked tumult and discord if kept the family of the Prophet captive. Thus, after almost eight days in captivity in the ruined house as prisoners, he called Imam al-Sajjad (p) and informed him that he was permitting them to return to Madina.

The growing rebukes and criticism frightened Yazid, even though most were sentiments expressed in private gatherings and bated tones. He directed Numan ibn Basheer along with a group of retainers from the Hashimites to prepare the captives for travel and instructed him to depart Damascus in secrecy and only

135. Al-Anwar al-Nu'mainiyya, Sayyid Nimatullah al-Jazairi, page 340

travel at night. Before giving them leave, Yazid summoned Imam Ali al-Sajjad (p) and feigned remorse and outright rejection of what he contended was done by ibn Ziyad, and informed him that he was permitting them to return to Madina. He said, "Tell me three desires that you would like fulfilled before your departure?" Imam al-Sajjad (p) replied, "The first is that you show me the face of my master and guardian Hussain so that I may benefit [from seeing him] and bid him farewell. The second is that you return to us our belongings that were plundered and taken from us. Lastly, if you desire to kill me, then dispatch a person who will take our women and children to the home of their grandfather." Yazid answered, "You will never look at the face of your father [again], and as for killing you, I have already abandoned wanting to do so. Therefore, no one other than yourself shall accompany the women to Madina. As for the belongings which were taken from you, I will give you more than that [in value]." The Imam then declared, "We do not want your wealth, it is sufficient for you (i.e., your worldly aspirations). I only ask that you return whatever was looted from us because it contains the hand-woven garments of Fatima, daughter of Muhammad, and her veil, necklace and shirt."[136] Yazid returned the belongings to Imam al-Sajjad (p) and also included 200 dinars, which the Imam distributed among the poor. As for the head of Imam Hussain (p), it is related that

---

136. al-Lahoof ala qatla al-tufoof, Sayyid ibn Tawoos, page 224

Yazid eventually gave in and allowed the captives to take it to be buried in Karbala.[137]

Arrival in Karbala

Zaynab (p) and the other released captives slowly traveled away from Damascus, they were now treated with a little more compassion than when they were taken prisoner. As they approached Iraq, they asked the travel guide to take them on a route that passes through Karbala on their way back to Madina. When they finally reached Karbala on the 20th of Safar, they saw that Jabir ibn Abdullah al-Ansari, the elderly companion of their grandfather the Prophet, was already there with a group of Hashimites.[138] Undoubtedly, each honorable lady must have rushed to the grave of her loved one after having been deprived of mourning them and visiting their graves, and the heartless way in which they were terrorized, tied up, and marched away from Karbala. Lady Layla bint Abi Murrah must have hurried to the grave of her son Ali al-Akbar, Lady Rabab bint Imri Qays must have gone to the grave of her six-month-old son Abdullah, and Lady Ramla would have fallen on the grave of her son Qasim. Maybe they all eventually went to the grave of Abbas, which was near the river, and solemnly remembered the

137. al-Lahoof ala qatla al-tufoof, Sayyid ibn Tawoos, page 225; Bihar al-Anwar, al-Majlisi, Vol. 45, page 140; Ilam al-Wara bi ilam al-Huda, al-Tabarsi, Vol. 1, page 477

138. al-Lahoof ala qatla al-tufoof, Sayyid ibn Tawoos, page 225

"moon of the Hashimites" and bringer of water. Each woman and child would have succumbed to the pent-up emotions that had been suppressed since the day of Ashura as the unbearable pain was released and the floodgates of tears opened.

Yet, how might Zaynab (p) have approached the grave of her beloved brother, particularly given everything she witnessed on the day of Ashura and the testament she carried on her shoulders after he was martyred in front of her eyes? As the severed head was returned to the grave, it might be that she remembered their days together as children in Madina. The inseparable brother and sister had a bond unlike any other siblings. Maybe she recounted the details of what happened to them after he was martyred, how they were robbed of their possessions, tied up and paraded in the streets of Kufah and Damascus. Certainly she must have told him that they faced innumerable insults and the crack of the whips as they were brought into the presence of ibn Ziyad and Yazid. Her brother would have known from being reunited in the next world, but she surely would have recounted to him what befell his daughter in the prison. Yet, Zaynab (p) must have also reassured her brother that she had fulfilled what he had asked her to do, which was to protect the living Imam, safeguard the other women and children, and preserve the legacy and dignity of the family of the Prophet.

The family of the Prophet remained in Karbala for three days mourning and commemorating the stand of their loved ones against the forces of tyranny and corruption. Indeed, this has been the inspiration for the millions of devotees who descend upon Karbala on the day of Arbaeen every year to remember the Master of the Martyrs and those who fought and died by his side. This tradition is rooted in the preservation of something sacred and is the means by which religious identity is passed from generation to generation. Thus, as the visitors approach Karbala on the 20th of Safar, they do so echoing the sentiments and strength of Zaynab, and declare their continuous adherence to his legacy. Moreover, it is a testament to the defense of humanity and everything that is pure and lofty. In the words of Jabir ibn Abdullah al-Ansari, "I heard the Messenger of God say, 'One who loves a [certain] group of people will be raised with them [on the Day of Judgement], and one who loves what they have achieved of deeds will share in [ther rewards].' By the One who sent Muhammad as a Prophet with the truth, my intention and that of my companions is the same as Hussain's and his companions who were all killed."[139]

---

139. Safeenatul Bihar, Abbas al-Qummi, Vol. 8, page 383

Chapter 9

························◆◆◆························

Back to Madina

A fter months away from the sanctuary of their grandfather, Zaynab (p) and the ladies of the Ahl al-Bayt (p) finally returned to Madina with the other captives. This must have been the most bittersweet of moments. As the caravan reached the outskirts of Madina, they stopped outside the city where they met Bishr ibn Hadhlam. Imam al-Sajjad (p) alighted from his camel and asked for the tents to be set up for some time. He then asked Bishr to enter Madina and announce the martyrdom of his father and those who were with him. It is reported that Bishr entered Madina and in a mournful voice declared, "O people of Yathrib! May you never encounter such a thing! Hussain is killed, so my tears now rain down! His body is in Karbala covered with blood, while his head is on a spear displayed [for all to see]". He then continued, "Here is Ali son of Hussain with his aunts and sisters, they have arrived back to you [in such a state], and I am his messenger who has come to inform you of their place."[140] The people began to rush out to

---

140. al-Lahoof ala qatla al-tufoof, Sayyid ibn Tawoos, page 227

the family of the Prophet. Bishr recounts, "There was no woman in Madina who did not come out wailing and mourning [upon hearing the news]. I did not see a greater number of mourners than on that day, nor a day of such sorrow since the death of the Messenger of God."[141]

It is reported that Imam al-Sajjad (p) then delivered a speech to the people of Madina in which he praised God and described his father's valor and their timeless stand. He also described how they were treated and what befell them at the hands of the enemy. Umm Kulthum advanced towards the gates of Madina and called out, "O city of our grandfather! You should not accept us, because we have come with sighs and grief! We left you accompanied by our family, and [now] we return to you with neither sons nor men." On the other hand, Zaynab (p) went straight to the grave of her grandfather and lamented, "I have come to announce to you the news of my brother Hussain's martyrdom and mourn his loss!" She would have recounted the ordeal they faced as she did at the grave of her brother. Maybe she told him, the mercy to all the worlds, of how mercilessly they were treated, and how his sunnah of kindness, compassion and gentleness, especially towards women, had been so heinously abandoned.

One would obviously conclude that Zaynab (p) secretly went to the grave of her mother. The way a child laments in the lap of her mother is unlike how she

---

141. al-Lahoof ala qatla al-tufoof, Sayyid ibn Tawoos, page 229

expresses her sorrow to anyone else. Thus, there is no real way to describe how Zaynab (p) must have acted when she finally approached the resting place of Lady Fatima. Could she have brought back the belongings of her brother and laid them down on the grave? Would she have described his brave fighting on the day of Ashura, or how he was finally martyred? Would she have recounted the way the enemy desecrated his body and robbed him of his possessions? Certainly, she must have told her that she fulfilled what was asked of her on the day of Ashura and afterwards. It is most appropriate that the answers to these questions be left to the personal feeling of empathy in the hearts of those who love Zaynab (p). This is underscored by the fact that she continued to mourn the loss of her brother and the other martyrs and keep their legacy alive, and thus, was not allowed to remain in the city of her grandfather to live out her remaining days in peace.

........••◆•◆•••........

Back to Sham and the Shrine of Lady Zaynab

Zaynab (p) continued to mourn the loss of her brother like her mother mourned for the Prophet in the remaining days of her life. The reader must certainly recognize that also like her mother, Zaynab's grave is not unanimously known. Although it is accepted to be in Damascus by the majority of Shia scholars, there are some who state that she is buried in Cairo, or even Madina. This shows the extent of animosity held by the Umayyads against the family of the Prophet. They went to great lengths to prevent Zaynab's persona from being revered and spared no effort to erase what she stood for and the symbol that she had become for the lovers of truth and justice.

After returning to Madina, Zaynab (p) did not remain silent or passively accept the atrocities committed by Yazid and his followers. Her words reminded the people of Madina of their pledge to the Prophet and fomented their anger and discontent towards the tyranny of the Umayyads. As the people began to question the authorities and demand for answers,

Yazid's appointed governor, Amru ibn Sad al-Ashdaq, sought his help and guidance, singling out Zaynab (p) as the cause of the discord and the threat to their rule. He was instructed to banish her from the city of her grandfather so that the people would not be able to hear her words or be moved by the greatness of her personality.

Historical reports indicate that Lady Zaynab (p) traveled to Egypt with some of the other ladies of the Prophet's family and remained there for a little over eleven months and eventually passed away and was buried there.[142] A shrine in her name exists until today in the Sayyida Zaynab neighborhood in the southern part of Cairo. On the other hand, more accepted reports, especially among the followers of Ahl al-Bayt (p), state that she moved with her husband to a property he owned on the outskirts of Damascus.[143] Unfortunately, the reason for this journey is still not entirely clear. Historians suggest that it might have been due to famine, which is unlikely due to a dearth in corroborating reports, expulsion, and even coercion. Regardless, she did not live long after the tragic events of Karbala and the calamities they faced in its aftermath. Lady Zaynab (p) became sick and left this world on the 15th of Rajab 62 A.H.

---

142. al-Tarikh, ibn Asakir, Vol. 13, page 39

143. Sayyida Zaynab, Sharif al-Qarashi, page 299

Epilogue

Today, there is a shrine over the grave of Lady Zaynab (p) in Damascus. Its beauty and splendor emanate from the grand character and spirit of this magnificent lady, who left a lasting imprint on human history. For this reason, thousands of lovers of truth and justice visit her shrine today and shed tears for her suffering. On the other hand, there is no such sentiment for the remnants of the Umayyads, whose despotic dynasty fomented hatred, prejudice, and the ruination of everything that is dignified and sacred. Even now, those who aspire to revive their evil ambitions and promote their devious ways against Islam, Prophet Muhammad (pbuh&hp) and his holy family have tried to assault her shrine in Damascus, just as they did the shrine of her brother in Karbala throughout history, but they are faced by the stalwart and undeterred lovers of the Ahl al-Bayt (p) who refuse to allow any harm to come to the legacy of this great lady and her memory.

The name Zaynab (p) is associated with dignity and courage; parents choose it for their daughters because it represents everything that is valuable and worthy and demonstrates the height of human achievement. The name Zaynab, just like Fatima, is synonymous with strength and resilience in the face of the most trying circumstances and hardship. It holds a special place in the hearts of Muslims, especially women, many of whom live through war, persecution, and other adversities, who flock to her grave from a young age and beseech, "O' Lady Zaynab, you are the beacon that has lit the path of righteousness for us. You are the indicator of piety, determination and resolve. Show us the means by which we can live a measure of how you lived, achieve what you achieved, speak out against tyranny and injustice by mimicking your powerful voice, and die with honor, with clear consciences, our heads held high, and leaving behind a legacy for those who follow."

Other publications from I.M.A.M.

Available for purchase online

- ❖ Advice to Youth
  By Grand Ayatullah Sayyid Ali al-Sistani
- ❖ Fasting: A Haven from Hellfire
  by Grand Ayatullah Sayyid Ali al-Sistani
- ❖ God's Emissaries: Adam to Jesus
  by Shaykh Rizwan Arastu
- ❖ Islam and Christianity: Brothers at Odds
  by Odeh Muhawesh
- ❖ Islamic Laws
  by Grand Ayatullah Sayyid Ali al-Sistani
- ❖ Islamic Laws of Expiations
  by Grand Ayatullah Sayyid Ali al-Sistani
- ❖ Islamic Laws of Death and Burial
  by Grand Ayatullah Sayyid Ali al-Sistani
- ❖ Islamic Laws of Food and Drink
  by Grand Ayatullah Sayyid Ali al-Sistani
- ❖ Who Is Hussain?
  by Dr. Mehdi Saeed Hazari
- ❖ Shia Muslims: Our Identity, Our Vision, and
  the Way Forward by Sayyid M. B. Kashmiri
- ❖ Tajwid: A Guide to Qur'anic Recitation
  by Shaykh Rizwan Arastu
- ❖ The Illuminating Lantern: An Exposition of
  Subtleties from the Quran
  by Shaykh Habib al-Kadhimi

Made in the USA
Columbia, SC
09 June 2025

59046026R00072